Emptying the Nest

Emptying the Nest

How to:
Launch Your Kids into Lives of their Own
Instill Security and Independence
Send Them Off and Keep Them as Friends
Feel Good About Yourself Through It All

Maryellen Walsh

PRENTICE
HALL
PRESS

New York   London   Toronto   Sydney   Tokyo   Singapore

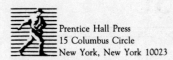Prentice Hall Press
15 Columbus Circle
New York, New York 10023

PRENTICE HALL PRESS and colophons are registered
trademarks of Simon & Schuster, Inc.

Library of Congress Cataloging-in-Publication Data

Walsh, Maryellen.
    Emptying the nest / Maryellen Walsh.
        p.   cm.
    Includes bibliographical references.
    ISBN 0-13-528191-1
    1. Young adults—United States.   2. Empty nesters—United States.
I. Title.
HQ799.7.W35   1990
305.23'5—dc20   90-37363
                                                      CIP

Designed by Richard Oriolo

Manufactured in the United States of America

10 9 8 7 6 5 4 3 2 1

First Edition

To my children, Douglas, Geoff, Stephen, and Lucy Hessel, and their spouses, Susan and Teri. Also to Robert Capps, Scot Small, and Geoffrey Small, star boarders in our house at one time or another.

Bon voyage, kids. Come back to port now and then.

Acknowledgments

Thanks to the many parents who took the time to answer my long questionnaire. They are: Susan Alden, Sandra Ashley, Nancy Baird, Mary Ann Baldridge, Janet Britton, Carolyn Buchanan, Jeanne Bundes, Barbara Charett, Debby Cohen, Meg Cole, Jimmi and Larry Dawson, Charlyne Dennis, Judy Edgar, Rhoda Eligator, Susan Ely, Tilly-Jo Emerson, Babette Feibel, Paula Folkman, Luella Goldberg, Linda Gross, Lu Hart, Joan Hawthorne, Leslie Holmes, Dixie Huefne, Barbara Johnson, Shirley Johnson, Phyllis Katz, Anne Kott, Mary Jane Levitch, Elizabeth Lourie, Carol Loysen, Lou Mason, Carol Nance, Margaret Newell, Joan Normington, Anne Richmond, Phyllis Ritvo, Nina Rodolitz, Mary Rogers, Nancy Sampson, Nancy Schonher, Ann Scott, Renata Selig, Margy Sharpe, Allene Soshea, Mary Taylor, Erin Van Speybroeck, Joan Viehoever, Susan Vrotsos, Sandra Williams, Mary Lou Winnick, and, of course, the ever-present Anonymous, of whom there were quite a few.

Other people were very helpful: Dodie Alexander, director of the Community Health Awareness Council; Mimi Bross, counselor at the Career Action Center; Sheldon Goldenberg, professor of sociology at the University of Calgary; Larry Lee, KRON-TV, Channel 4, San Francisco; June Lim from the Career Planning and Placement Center at San Jose State University; Tom Reefe from the Career Center at the University of California, Santa Cruz; Krista Resing, KRON-TV, Channel 4, San Francisco; and Allan Schnaiberg, professor of sociology and urban affairs at Northwestern University.

Every author owes a debt to those who have gone before. In this case, Jean Okimoto and Phyllis Stegall paved the way for this book with *Boomerang Kids*, a look at what happens and should happen when the young adult returns home. No doubt many parents owe these two women a tip of the hat for their suggestions about how to make two-generational living work.

Thanks also to Dana DiCroce, Rosemary Hopkins, Ann Kenworthy, Ruth Sherer, Dave Soares, and Terry Wright.

I'm grateful as well to those who reviewed the first draft of the manuscript: Tom and Maureen Blakeslee, Elaine and Larry Dohan, John and Aileen Hessel, Louis and Lucille Santoro, and John and Nancy Snyder. Thus did I try to consumer-test this book.

A special debt is owed to Robert Taylor, M.D., who generously evaluated the text whenever and wherever it touched on medical issues. Also shoring up the medical side and offering many an insight about the relationships between generations is Reed Kaplan, M.D., former head of inpatient psychiatry at Stanford University Medical Center.

Thanks go to my editor at Prentice Hall, Gail Winston, and to my agent, Peter Ginsberg of Curtis Brown, Ltd.

A final thank-you to Mac Small, the last of the gentlemen lawyers.

Contents

Contents

Contents

Foreword

A Necessary Perspective

The foreword of a book presents a choice to the reader: to read it or not to read it? . . . that's the question. The answer here is read it, because in this foreword the reader will discover at least two myths about the empty nest that need to be put to rest.

The first myth is that the last stage of parenting must necessarily be loaded with conflict and resentment, with the parent shoving, the offspring resisting, and the nest being the scene of a battle royal. The truth is that parents and kids do not have to wage an all-out war for independence. Yes, there may be skirmishes and small-scale police actions, but nuclear weapons are not usually necessary to empty the nest. Instead, in this book, you will find many ways to make this last parental engagement with young adult sons and daughters both pleasant and rewarding.

The second myth is that the younger generation's returning home is a new phenomenon on the demographic map—a blip nouveau, statistically speaking. According to this mistaken view, today's young adults are an unprecedented generation, living, as they often do, with their parents for a while and then marrying later than their mothers and fathers.

Instead, the truth is that we parents were the exceptions, the statistical oddity, at least in this century. In contrast to our parents and our kids, we who came of age in the 1950s and 1960s left home and married young. In 1956, the median marriage age for men was twenty-two, and for women, twenty. Historically, these are the youngest marriage ages on record for the United States. Our generation, in other words, left the nest early.

But Americans before us did not rush out of the nest as we did. In fact, around 1900, fully one-third of the population never married. Those were the bachelor great uncles who lived in the old homestead as adults and the maiden great aunts who stayed home and "helped." Even in 1940, right after the Depression, a hefty 43 percent of young adults, ages eighteen to twenty-nine, were living at home. So it can be argued that today's young adults are simply following a tradition that was interrupted by our generation—we who had babies before our acne cleared, we who fled the nest, so that by 1960, only 22.7 percent of young adults between ages eighteen and thirty-four lived at home.

After us, though, the demographic tide turned again toward young people living at home. By 1983, according to Dr. David Heer in "The Cluttered Nest," the percentage of young people living with their parents went back up, this time to 30.3 percent. Recent surveys put today's numbers even higher. According to the *New York Times*, 51 percent of single men ages twenty to twenty-four and 34 percent of single women in that same age group are living with their parents.

How can we make sense of these changes? Why were we the ones to leave home early, and why did those before us and those after us take their time? Why will one generation leave home early and another stay in the nest longer? Nobody really knows, but most observers relate the phenomenon to the economy.

When the economy is relatively benign, unemployment low, and jobs plentiful, it is easier for young people to leave home and set up their own nests. On the other hand, when the economy is harsh and jobs are hard to get, the number of young people in the nest will rise.

Psychiatrist Dr. Reed Kaplan puts these trends in another perspective. He views the ebb and flow of the age of independence as natural behavior on the part of the human animal. In stressful times, when the environment is less hospitable, the tendency of the human animal is to stick close to home. On the other hand, says Dr. Kaplan, exploratory behavior increases as the environment grows more benign. Experiments with monkeys have shown this relationship between the environment and nest-leaving behavior to be true. It certainly is possible that human populations behave similarly.

To look at the nest, empty or not, from an economic or biological perspective is not only illuminating but liberating. It frees parents and kids alike from the tyranny of censure, from thinking it is "awful" that today's kids are still at home. If a longer time at home is seen as a natural response to economic forces, as an adaptive response to a harsh outside environment, critical judgments tend to diminish. So does blaming oneself or one's kids for taking "extra" time to grow up.

When wondering, then, why your kids aren't out of the nest, remember that it is a tough world, especially today. Competition for jobs, housing, and mates is fierce. Don't be surprised, therefore, if your nest is used as a refuge, at least until the young adult gets a foothold in the world.

How This Book Can Help

What this book offers is a way to make that final time of parenting work so that the young person, though perhaps still at home, is helped to become a capable and competent adult. If you have a kid in college—or one who has graduated from college but not from you—you can probably use this book to help you find your way. Most of us parents can use a little guidance as we coach our kids toward independent adulthood.

Emptying the nest sounds simple enough in theory: When the kids finally get out of school, just cut the apron strings. One snip and the son or daughter is out of the nest, and mom and dad are once more the rulers of the critical realms of the house—those fought-over domestic territories known as the refrigerator, the phone, and the TV set.

But the 36 million American parents with young adults

still at home know that emptying the nest is not simple. The rules have changed when it comes to their adult offspring growing up and leaving home. So parenthood, stage two, can be confusing, especially when it comes to sharing quarters with adult kids.

Living at home, however, is not the only issue that puzzles parents. Parental involvement often continues even though sons and daughters have moved away. The kids may have a new address, but there are still ways that parents can and do contribute to their kids' start-and-stop lurch toward adulthood. For instance, though living on their own, sons and daughters often need and want nonintrusive coaching about vital life choices: careers, for one, handling money and credit, for another.

However, when it comes to coaching the kids toward independence, we parents may be offering old advice in a new game. Times have changed so much in the last few decades that we parents can no longer assume that older is wiser. Much of what we "know" is out of date: Our familiar world slipped out from under us while we were busy raising kids. For instance, think about the advice we may offer about careers. Is our advice Stone Age or Space Age when it comes to getting jobs? Are we up to date when discussing careers with our kids? Are we flexible or are we still trying to push every kid in the country into medical school?

But there's help available when it comes to handling these issues. In this book, for example, you'll find specific information on kids' careers along with pointers about a spectrum of other concerns vital to their independence. It may not be simple anymore, this growing up business, but we can help each other learn what we need to know to launch our kids.

Foreword

So, if you want to nudge your kids toward independence, if you hope someday to reclaim the unalienable right to the volume controls of the stereo, if you wish to finish parenting before senility sets in, read on. Enjoy the book and remember this comforting irony about parenthood: Parenthood may, even should, be terminal, but it is not fatal. No one has ever died from a severed apron string.

—MARYELLEN WALSH

I would there were no age between sixteen and three and twenty, or that youth would sleep out the rest; for there is nothing in between but getting wenches with child, wronging the ancientry, stealing, fighting.

—SHAKESPEARE
The Winter's Tale

Being constantly with the children was like wearing a pair of shoes that were expensive and too small. She couldn't bear to throw them out, but they gave her blisters.

—BERYL BAMBRIDGE
Injury Time

How hard it is to let the kids go and how wrong it is not to.

—A FATHER
JOHN SNYDER, M.D.

. . . and the parents left town with no forwarding address. . . .

—URBAN FOLKTALE
UNITED STATES OF AMERICA

1

Leaving the Nest

Why This Book?

Most people think kids leave the nest when they go to college. Not so. College is independence with training wheels.

The real action starts postcollege. That's when the caps and gowns go back to the rental agency and the kids come home. They sleep. They eat. They flip moodily through the help-wanted ads, wondering how to reconcile their hopes of being rock stars with their degrees in English.

And hovering over these postcollege days is the parental expectation that someday our children will become a Joe Montana, a Lee Iacocca, the president—or, preferably, all three in cleverly planned strategic order. Mind you we par-

1

ents never actually say this Joe Montana, Lee Iacocca stuff. No, the official statement of enlightened parents everywhere is, "Be anything you want. We just want you to be happy." And we parents believe we mean it when we say it.

I've emptied the nest of three sons, one daughter, and several other live-in young people. I've learned much about what to do and what not to do, mostly by tripping over my own good intentions until I found ways that worked, ways that will be passed on to you in the pages to come. I have also, when appropriate, interviewed experts for this book—psychiatrists, youth counselors, sociologists, drug and alcohol experts, career advisors—to bring you a more complete picture of the growing-up process.

This book, however, is also firmly grounded by the lives of many parents whom I've interviewed either in person or by questionnaire. Each of these parents had one or more postcollege young adults. About half of them had adult kids living at home. Their response to the survey, then, was grounded in real experience, not in theory. Each took the time to answer questions about kids living at home, getting jobs, handling money, setting up their own nests, using drugs and alcohol, and getting along with the rest of the family.

These parents responded generously, as if they instinctively sensed they were talking about an important process. It *is* important, for producing a competent, self-sufficient adult is one of nature's essential tasks. Isn't it crucial, then, that we parents learn how to coach our offspring not in Little League baseball but in Major League living; that is, surviving in a world that is often unfair, disappointing, and confusing? So that's why this book was written, as a guide for perplexed parents who struggle with problems such as these:

• *Living at Home.* Deborah felt like a has-been at twenty-five. Laid off from her first job, she was out of money and couldn't pay the rent on her apartment. She asked if she could live at home for a while. Her parents said yes, and Deborah arrived home with her furniture, her cat, her records, and a tattered ego. She now fights with her parents about dishes in the sink and smoking in her room. A big blowup is on the horizon about whether or not her boyfriend can stay overnight. What can be done to head off a family collision? Chapter 2, "Living at Home," presents ways to solve such problems and to make living back home for a while work.

• *Getting the First Job.* Brad graduated from college, came home, and went into hiding. He and his compact disc player got to know each other very well. He wrote a resume. Then rewrote it. And then changed it ten times more. His father grumped that Brad was hung up on writing the great American resume. Brad's mother left the morning paper on the dining room table, delicately folded to the help-wanted section. Brad was more interested in the sports section. He just would not get off the dime and hunt for a job. What can his parents do about it? That question and many others related to the first job-hunting efforts of young adults will be answered in chapter 3, "Getting the First Job." After reading it, parents should have enough up-to-date information about the employment arena to become informed allies and effective coaches in their young adult's search for a full-time job.

• *Money and the Necessities of Living.* Twenty-two-year-old Bob asked his parents to cosign his application for a major credit card. He also needed help with the first and last month's rent and the security deposit for a new apartment. Are his requests out of line? Also, Bob's place of work doesn't offer medical insurance. Should his parents help? Chapter 4 discusses money and other necessities of living, such as cars and apartments. This chapter also provides a framework for deciding what kinds of financial help, if any, are reasonable to provide.

• *Trouble.* Trouble with young adult sons and daughters can arrive wearing many faces. Sharon's parents noticed that Sharon couldn't hold a job for more than three months. She was perpetually broke and growing thinner every month. They were worried, no doubt about it. And then they got the call from the hospital. The pieces fell into place. Sharon was being treated for an overdose of cocaine. Problems with drugs, alcohol, and mental disorders are often why kids won't and can't move into independent adulthood. Chapter 5, "Trouble Time," tells how to recognize these common problems and what to do about them.

• *Family Relations.* George and Helen found themselves at odds with their adult kids on a variety of subjects. They didn't like their son's choice of a girlfriend and didn't let him forget it. Helen had a series of arguments with her daughter over her daughter's wedding. They tangled over everything from the shape of the champagne glasses to the color of the bridesmaids' gowns. And George was getting highly competitive with his son, whose professional success threatened to eclipse his father's. Both kids complained that Helen and George never respected their choices or accomplishments. Chapter 6, "Kidiquette: Manners for the Modern Parent," gives pointers on how to resolve some of these common glitches in family relations.

Now let's look at the context in which we live with

our kids . . . the social and economic background affecting much of what we do and think. For only when we understand our surroundings can we begin to understand ourselves and our families.

So How Come They Can't Leave Home Like We Did?

Parents seem to be mystified, resentful, even angry over the fact that this generation can't just leave home, get a job, get married, and grow up. We did it in the fifties and sixties, and it was no big deal. Why does it seem to be so hard for our children?

Because the world changed when we weren't looking.

Because the rules aren't the same.

Here are some of the differences between then and now. To understand and acknowledge them makes it easier to navigate as a parent.

Let's begin with the basics: the human sexual drive. Previous generations had to leave home and get married to find sexual fulfillment because sex was sanctified only within marriage. In the old days, if you wanted a full sex life, hated to have a guilty conscience, and were anxious about pregnancy, you got married. That was it. And almost all of us who are now parents of young adults got married in our early twenties. The natural drives of the mating game served to propel us away from our parental home and into our own.

Then came reliable birth control in the form of a pill and the rules changed. Sex outside of marriage could be accomplished much more easily once the likelihood of pregnancy was removed. Young people didn't have to get married and leave home to have sexual relations. They could find sex partners in high school, college, work, all over. So an important biological propellant to independence had greatly diminished. Sex was no longer a reason to leave home or grow up.

Another basic change lay in the pocketbook rather than in the bedroom. The dollar doesn't buy what it used to. Look, for example, at housing costs. (Since people can't leave home without having another home to jump to, housing costs are directly relevant to the process of clearing out of the family home.) In a nutshell, housing costs have skyrocketed. A starter house in some high-priced urban areas can cost as much as $200,000.

Just translate that housing price tag into financial reality. A $200,000 house would normally require $20,000 down and a mortgage payment of about $1,800 a month, assuming a mortgage rate of 10 percent. To qualify for a mortgage of $180,000, a lender would not uncommonly require a monthly income of about $5,400, or three times the house payment.

What young person earns $5,400 a month at an entry-level job? Almost none. It's not an entry-level salary except in high-priced professions like law and medicine. Many people just out of college might start at around $20,000 to $25,000 a year, which is less than half of what's required to buy a starter house, at least in high-ticket urban areas. (Your children may live in a place where housing is more reasonable. But more reasonable still often means unaffordable to the young person just starting out.)

So, you can see why your children aren't running out and buying themselves their own home sweet home. They can't afford it. They often can't even afford rent, which is, of course, the economic reality that sends them back home to you.

Perhaps the fact that housing costs have skyrocketed is a self-evident truth to you. If so, congratulate yourself. You're up-to-date. But some of us parents are still paying ridiculously low monthly payments on thirty-year-old 5-percent mortgages, or we haven't rented a place in twenty years, so we may be out of touch with the new realities. If you feel you need updating, read the real estate ads for your area. They will get you up-to-speed fast.

Still other forces besides inflation, tighter housing, and freer sex keep young people from leaving the nest. One factor is rarely acknowledged but definitely present: the seductive living standard of well-to-do parents. Some midlife parents have accumulated many material goodies: comfortable houses, swimming pools, gardens, garages filled with expensive cars—all likely to be located in safer and prettier neighborhoods than their young adult offspring can afford. This upscale kind of parental home is tempting to cling to, when all the younger generation can often get is a cramped apartment in a neighborhood with a high crime rate. With such a contrast, who wouldn't want to stay home? Far fewer of us had parents who lived on such a lush scale, so we weren't tied to our family homes with golden apron strings.

Those then, are just some of the differences between then and now. Acknowledging these changes as we deal with our offspring will go a long way in helping us understand rather than judge the young folks we brought into the world. If you remember one basic truth—*that* was then and *this* is

7

now—you have mastered part of what it takes to be a parent who can launch offspring successfully.

Is There One Right Way to Grow Up?

Of course not.

But we mothers and fathers sometimes behave as if there were a sacred timetable written in the sky, a universal growing-up schedule similiar to the one we obeyed twenty or thirty years ago. Here's how that schedule often runs in our expectations, and what we may want our offspring to do:

- Finish a four-year college by twenty-one or twenty-two, at the very outside
- Get a job, preferably one a parent can brag about
- Get an apartment with a "darling" roommate, one who stands when mother comes into the room
- Move all personal remnants out of family home, including baseball trophies, old skis, and high school yearbooks
- Get married to someone who looks like Jimmy Stewart or Debbie Reynolds
- Buy a house
- Have two babies: one boy, one girl

Those who follow this schedule, *our* schedule, we officially certify as grown-ups. The rest, the thirty-four-year-old bachelor son, the daughter who won't "settle down," these kids-who-are-not-kids somehow arouse uneasiness and suspi-

cion in parental breasts. After all, when we were their age—
et cetera, et cetera.

Well, as noted in the Foreword, we are the demographic exceptions, the ones who broke tradition by marrying earlier than any other generation in the United States.
So we shouldn't proceed on the assumption that our timetable must be carried out by our children. There is no univer-
sally correct schedule for growing up. Those who nudge their
offspring toward the life patterns of the fifties or sixties might
consider easing up. As a friend of mine says, "Don't push
the river; it flows by itself."

Now let's shift from looking at our socioeconomic background to considering some practical rules for the smooth
launching of sons and daughters into the world.

What Parents Need to Know

Some parents present the appearance of perfection when it
comes to the launching of children. They seem, at least to
the rest of us who sometimes stumble, to possess some magic
touch. Their children appear to grow up effortlessly, no seam
showing between adolescence and adulthood. No difficulties
with school, drugs, sex, alcohol, jobs, or identity for these
families. In our envying imaginations, at least, these perfect
parents produce only neurosurgeons and astronauts.

Well, the truth is that these fictional paragons do not
exist. We who have problems—and who does not?—simply
imagine that the grass is greener in other families. We fall
for this myth because there are, in fact, occasional people
whose egos push them to pretend to the rest of us that their

family life is wonderful, their marriage is made in heaven, their children are pure joy. (Mostly these domestic state-of-the-union messages come in long holiday cards.)

But don't chase this impossible dream and don't berate yourself for not being perfect. You are doing well if you have only wanted to kill your children 5 percent of the time. And vice versa.

So having disposed of the ideal, let's get down to reality. Just what does it take for a parent to give a great good-bye? What's needed to become a benign nest-buster, a friendly apron-string cutter? Are there some general tips to be learned about the noble goal of sending sons and daughters forth into the world?

Yes.

And the first is this . . .

Independence Starts at Zero

Independence doesn't happen all of a sudden. It's not a kind of Fourth of July of the human spirit, where overnight, midst flares and fireworks, an adult is born. Instead, growing up is an evolutionary process that we parents should prepare our kids for long before the time of launch. As one mother told me, "It all begins at age zero."

Again and again, parents who had launched their children said that independence should be fostered throughout childhood by treating sons and daughters not as extensions of the parents or as cute "things" but as valuable people— young and inexperienced people to be sure, but people, nonetheless, who are given responsibilities along with opportunities to develop independence as they're growing up.

For instance, young people should be encouraged to venture from home long before they leave for college. One parent noted, "We have always encouraged short departures—summer camp, summer jobs away from home, going to visit relatives." Clearly, these expeditions help young people learn to be on their own.

Some of the most exciting experiences of early childhood—for example, camping out overnight in the backyard—are really early experiments with independence. In pup tents, children learn the courage to handle the lions and tigers and bears of the darkened yard, building confidence in their ability to survive, removed from the magic circle of the family. It may be just a backyard at night, the child may be just seven years old, but the experience is a useful one—and for the parents, too, who are learning to let go.

Independence, however, can also be successfully practiced without stepping out the front door. For instance, in our family we targeted the senior year of high school as "semi-going-it-alone-time." In that last year at home I dropped the role of parent/supervisor. I was to step in only if a disaster loomed (someone drinking and driving) or I was truly inconvenienced (late parties). Otherwise, my sons and daughter had control of what they were going to do, when they were going to do it, and with whom. The buck stopped with them. Parental restraints were removed, with minor exceptions such as letting the rest of us know if they weren't going to be home for dinner and being responsible for household chores. Mainly, though, my offspring were, in their senior year of high school, president and chief operating officers of themselves.

The system worked well for us, since it provided freedom in an environment where the reins were light, but there if needed. Though I can't prove it, my feeling is that my kids did better in college than they would have had we held on tightly until departure day. University freshmen may get in trouble if there is too great a gap between the rules of home and the freedoms of college. In our family we tried to narrow that gap so the adjustment wasn't so difficult or disaster-prone. I never developed a formal name for this way of treating the senior year of high school. Maybe it's just ratcheting kids into adulthood, notch by notch.

Now let's go to the next important point about launching sons and daughters. . . .

Moral Support: Lifeblood of a Launch

Again and again in the surveys I sent out one word was repeated. *Support. Support. Support.* That, to parents, is an essential ingredient in the launching process. Exactly what do they mean by this word? And how is support translated into everyday actions?

Support means encouragement, a kind of benign parental coaching that gets across the important message that we believe in you. We may not agree with every decision you make, but we are with you.

Playing these supporting roles, we find ourselves both cheerleaders and coaches. But note that cheering for your offspring does not mean pretending to go along with decisions you can't in your heart agree with. If my daughter decided to become a Broadway actress, I would not like it and would tell her so. (My father was a Broadway producer, so I know that life in the theater can be brutal.) However, having expressed my concerns and reservations, I would help my daughter in every way possible, from editing her resume to steering her to the acting jobs that put bread on the table.

So support does not always mean expressing agreement. In fact, it often means encouraging the young adult in an effort that is simply foreign to the parents. My surveys are full of examples of parents stretching their sympathies to encourage their children in professions the parents either knew nothing about or with which they felt uncomfortable.

For instance, there was a couple, both college professors, whose son went into the management of pizza parlors. They had to stretch their habitual values to include their son's interests. They didn't waste time wishing he were a Rhodes scholar. Instead, they respected his individual inclination, even if it led to business rather than books.

Another mother and father—understated sorts who loved nature and classical music—were horrified when their daughter joined a rock band. They, however, changed their tune when she actually began earning money with her gigs. The parents came around and now invite her to perform for their friends.

Not all stories have such happy endings. Families trip over this issue of accepting what the son or daughter wants to do, because the life path chosen is simply alien to the parents and to the expectations and interests of their particular home. You may have noticed that some homes are held together by mutual interests. Similar inclinations in hobbies or professions are the glue of the family unit. There are sports-nut families, math families, and families where music

13

is the uniting factor. There are education-oriented families held together by SAT scores, and families where almost everybody is in medicine, or social work, or retail. There are, sadly, even families where the common interest is drugs or alcohol.

But into these family clusters, mavericks are born all the time, sons or daughters who just don't buy the accepted program. It is not necessarily because they are rebelling, but often because the family program just doesn't interest them. These differing values can cause family tensions if the parents don't rearrange their vision of life to include the enthusiasms of their children, however odd they seem.

So, support by encouraging, even if you don't feel a gut sympathy for what your son or daughter wants to do. If it is difficult for you, remember how sad it is when humans waste their lives because they don't do what they really want. Self-esteem and pride can be eaten away by too many compromises between what we want to be and what society thinks we should be. If there's only one life to lead, it shouldn't be lived by someone who isn't really us.

As one father said, "I figure I had my turn to do what I wanted and now it's our son's turn. He wants to work in a dead-end job in public-interest law. Long hours. Low pay. I wouldn't do it, but it's his life. I'm not happy about his decision, but I leave him alone on the subject. He's doing what he wants."

And one mother said, "My daughter is a hairdresser. I wanted something more for her . . . to have what I didn't have . . . to do something more—well—professional. We told her that just once and she got mad. She said she helps people feel great about themselves and she thinks she does as much good in the world as a psychiatrist. Actually, she's super at what she does and I go to her and she does make me look and feel great. It took a while, but I can see why she likes what she does."

So give your children the freedom to be who they really are.

Another essential element of support is listening. Listening well is perhaps the most endearing attribute any parent can have. It's a kind of focused attentiveness that is irresistible. If you have this ability to listen, your family is lucky.

But, ironically, part of listening is talking—asking thoughtful, nonthreatening questions that draw out the essence of what happened and how the other person feels about it. Also useful are questions that gently prod your offspring to figure out how they are going to handle whatever situation they are in as they set out on their own.

To that end, when your offspring are in a confusing bind, perhaps during a discouraging job hunt, have them ask themselves these three basic clarifying questions:

1. What is happening?
2. What do I want to happen?
3. How am I going to make it happen?

These three questions, asked and answered, are the way out of many a predicament. The answer to the first question—what is happening?—describes the problem. The answer to the second—what do I want to happen?—defines the goal. The answer to the third—how am I going to make it happen?—outlines the means of reaching the goal.

I have used this technique for twenty years: It has never failed to help solve confusing dilemmas. Try it yourself. Pass it on to your family. Writing the answers out is especially useful.

Yet another way to become a Pulitzer prize–winning ear is to reflect back to your sons and daughters what they've said. Reflecting back thoughts and feelings is an excellent way of letting them know you are really paying attention. For example, your son has just told you how frustrated he is about having mailed fifty resumes and having received zero answers. You can let your son know you understand by saying something such as, "I see you're frustrated and I don't blame you. I would be, too."

Then you can go on to tell him how nobody ever answered your resumes thirty years ago either. Ironically, stories of parental failure can have a very positive effect on our children. It makes them feel they're not alone. In fact, I think my offspring actually like to hear stories of how many times my first book got rejected before it was published, or how I cried at the kitchen table over the want ads when I couldn't get a job as a newly divorced, midlife mom trying to switch careers. I guess being transparent about our personal adversities is somehow reassuring. It lets us know we're all humans in the same leaky boat of life.

So listen, and share some of your war stories.

Don't Make a Career of Rescuing Your Offspring

When discussing the younger generation in an interview for this book, sociologist Dr. Allan Schnaiberg said, "My core bet is that this [younger] generation wasn't prepared to deal with risk and failure. We were the first generation of parents who had both the motive and means to rescue our kids. So when trouble does come, the kids have difficulty confronting both loss and failure."

He may be right. If every time our kids get in trouble or make a mistake, we rush to their rescue, we are doing them a great disservice. Not a little disservice, but a big one. Overhelping actually handicaps them by interfering with their ability to lead successful, self-directed lives.

Most of us know intellectually that our children will never learn if rescued constantly from the consequences of their mistakes. We've lived long enough to observe that goofing, bungling, fumbling, and blundering are wonderful ways to learn. Trying and making mistakes—that's how we figure out what will work for us in life and what won't. Good judgment comes from experience, but valuable experience comes from misjudgment, making a mistake. No pain, no gain.

Even though our wise selves know that constant rescue work destroys rather than saves, why can't we just say no to the son who now needs a loan to pay his rent because he blew all his money on a vacation to Puerto Vallarta last month? Why do we sometimes step in to rescue when we know we shouldn't?

Blame biology. Protecting and helping our offspring is a basic in-the-genes drive. We are biologically programmed to ward off danger when it comes to our kids. It's that simple. We are like bears protecting their cubs, lionesses standing guard by their little lionettes.

On the other hand, we as a species have had to learn to tame similar basic impulses. For instance, though richly programmed to mate and reproduce, we don't grab attractive people on the street and mate with them in the middle of the sidewalk. We've been socialized to curb our sex drive and now our species displays it pretty much only in limited, private situations—office parties being, perhaps, a notable exception.

To bring up our children to be independent, we have to learn to subdue and control our protective instincts too. Shielding our children from the unpleasant consequences of their actions and not letting them make mistakes is biology run amok. Our sons and daughters must be allowed to stumble along and find their way without us always running interference.

Parent voices are strong on this subject according to my surveys:

"Don't rescue them all the time from the pickles they get into."

"If you spoil them by making their way forever smooth, they won't learn how to cope."

"Let them make their own mistakes."

What's being said here is, don't make a habit of rescuing. This is not to say we should *never* rescue. In fact, we would be hard-hearted and setting a bad example if we refused to occasionally pull them out of the drink.

So how do we judge when it's okay to help and when it isn't? How do we know when bailing out our kids will help them grow up and when it will stunt them?

The First Mistake Rule

By trial and error, I've evolved the First Mistake Rule, which goes like this: If a son or daughter gets in trouble and needs help, give aid unstintingly the first time. Be reluctant the second time, and sign off on the third.

And the rescuing that does go on has a string attached: a mandatory discussion between parent and child. But blaming doesn't help a lot here: Problem-solving is more productive. For instance, if a daughter with her first credit card runs up a bill that is beyond her means, you may want to rescue her in the form of a loan or gift before she ruins her nascent credit. But this handout should have a discussion attached, perhaps some pointers on budgeting or actually working out a budget, maybe sharing how you yourself avoid getting buried under department store bills, or how you resist the temptation to spend.

But if the same thing keeps happening month after month, sign off. She's got a problem that she has to learn how to address. Getting her credit cut off will teach her fiscal responsibility quite efficiently.

Or, say, a son borrows your car and returns it with the gas tank on empty, so empty that you have to hold your breath driving to the gas station for a refill. To me, that's a clear situation. Talk to him, and if it keeps happening, no more loaning your car.

The First Mistake Rule makes a lot of sense since it allows some leeway for the very human part of ourselves that likes to test accepted ways of doing things. Observing myself and my offspring for several decades, I can say that we are curious creatures and will try things once, even things we "know" we shouldn't do. Often, it's not until we see how we feel after we've done it that we know it's not for us.

Just think, for instance, of the enduring ethical issues—the times when people wonder if it's okay to cheat on exams, taxes, or spouses. Often a one-time experiment and the resulting guilt, remorse, and negative consequences quickly teach us that the low road is no road to take. I stole a pair of knitting needles—for their beautiful ivory color and smooth texture—when I was in the third grade. I never took anything again. Knowing I was the knitting needle thief of Camp Kilmer, New Jersey, was too much of a torment for my nine-year-old conscience. Besides, I didn't know how to knit.

So, my utter lack of perfection helps me retain a tolerant view of first offenses. There are, however, parents who go on being tolerant after third, fourth, and fifth offenses. Why can't these parents just say no and leave the rest to the great teacher in the sky, negative experience?

We've already suggested that instinct has a lot to do with overrescuing: We're programmed to protect our cubs. But there are other reasons why we hang on by helping too much. For instance, single parents may find themselves rescuing constantly because they feel guilty over their divorce. They just can't set limits. And sometimes parents who themselves had extremely strict parents swing to the other end of the pendulum and are permissive to the point of handicapping their kids.

Then, too, there are the parents who haven't had much love in their lives. Perhaps they were abused or neglected by their own parents. Sometimes these underloved people, now parents themselves, feel they're risking the love they've come to enjoy with their children by telling those children no.

In still other cases, parents who need to be needed or in control may overhelp their offspring. Money is an especially effective way of holding on. He who pays the piper calls the tune, and the parent who always plays the role of walking wallet has more control over the kids than one who lets them learn about money and credit the hard way.

As Other Parents See It: Predictable Obstacles to Leaving the Nest

One surprise hit me as I read the parent surveys. When asked what was the biggest obstacle to the launching of children, the most common answer was . . . *parents*. (And this opinion was from parents.)

Most of the replies zeroed in on one specific point: Parents can and do mess up their kids' independence by not making their children responsible for their own lives. Otherwise bright and well-meaning mothers and fathers can completely miss the fact that some young adults are reluctant to take over their own helms. They want mommy and daddy to steer for them. Some parents go along with this inappropriate dependence, assuming it is still their job to make life "nice" for offspring a quarter century old. Some adult offspring still think it's mom and dad's job to provide a protective shield against the economic and emotional realities of the world. Why do some parents willingly continue as shepherds, guards, defenders, buffers, and chancellors of the exchequer?

Because it's been the parent role for some twenty years. Because many of us forget to hand in our resignation papers as parents when our kids hit adulthood. One woman told me this story: "Our twenty-two-year-old son had been out of college for nine months and still did not have a job. He had offers closely related to what he wanted to do, but to our astonishment and disapproval he turned them down. One day we had a heart-to-heart talk. I told him that I thought it was time to take a job, even if it wasn't the perfect one. He looked at me in a wounded way. " 'You're killing my dream,' " he said.

She continued, "It took me a year after that to figure out what I should have said. (I'm not too swift on these issues.) I should have told him (and myself) that an adult is responsible for pursuing his own dream. I don't hold him responsible for my dreams, and he shouldn't hold me responsible for his." Parents need to know this in their souls: Children are responsible for their own lives, just as we are responsible for ours. Recognizing ultimate responsibility doesn't mean we can't lend each other a hand now and then, but it does mean that the buck for their lives stops with them.

Respondents to the survey were strong on this issue too:

"Make them do things for themselves."

"Parents should insist sons and daughters be responsible for themselves."

"Be there, but don't rescue."

It's a Jungle Out There

Taking another tack on the question of obstacles to growing up, respondents zeroed in on the nature of today's work world. After saying that parents were the biggest barrier to their kids getting launched in life, they named the job market as the second biggest obstacle. They saw the work world as a confusing, complex, and competitive place that can frighten and discourage fledgling adults who don't understand the rules, the game, the players, or even where the playing field is.

Parents said:

"It's too difficult to determine career direction these days."

"There's too much professional choice."

"How can anybody understand this job market, where to go, what to be? As a reentry woman, I can't figure it out myself, and I'm presumably wiser than my young son."

"Finding your life work is hard."

"Too much competition is a huge obstacle. Our generation didn't have to face this much pressure."

"There is not enough career knowledge. So many new kinds of jobs have appeared. I read the want ads and don't understand what the job titles mean."

"Our society doesn't have institutionalized ways of helping people find jobs, so people are left on their own."

These comments seem on target. When I was pondering "careers," I felt that there were exactly four life paths open to me: mother, teacher, nurse, and secretary. Today, my daughter can be a courtroom litigator, an architect, an anesthesiologist, a pilot, a marketing manager, or almost anything she wants. We've come far. There are now so many kinds of jobs that we no longer know the names of them all.

This confusing job market is a real obstacle to the successful launching of a young adult. The next chapter is specifically geared to provide concrete, practical help to you who are the coaches of your about-to-be-employed sons and daughters. Remember, the goal is to teach them to catch fish themselves rather than to fish for them.

A Few Final Pains in the Parental Neck

According to the parent surveys, there are even more obstacles to leaving the nest. The first is kids' fear of disappointing their parents and themselves. But there is a solution for readers whose sons and daughters may be frozen on the spot by the fear of failure. It's a technique I've used successfully on myself and on my kids, who will now try any work experience, even if they are sometimes a little nervous around the edges.

Fear of failure means that whoever is overwhelmed by the emotion is simply afraid of making a mistake. The solution is to eliminate negative thinking about mistakes and all the lacerating self-judgments that ride along with it.

Invite your offspring to do the same. Think instead that things either work or they don't work. If they do work, great. If they don't work, figure out why not and take that information to try something else. Don't cry or fret or self-flagellate. Something simply did not work. Big deal. And with this no-such-thing-as-a-bad-mistake idea under your philosophical belt, you can enjoy life as if you were playing an intriguing kind of learning game. And pass on these ideas to your kids for their consideration. It will be a tremendous relief to them if they are now struggling with the fear of goofing up their newly minted adult lives.

For instance, if after enrolling in law school your son

finds out that spending all day wrestling with the written contractual word is as unpleasant as a jail sentence, then tell him to declare that particular professional move something that didn't work, not an awful mistake. And encourage him to let the next professional try involve an occupation that doesn't require close attention to written detail.

Another way to diminish the fear of failure is to teach your offspring to make worst-case game plans. As they ponder a move in life—say taking a job they are not sure of—they can ask themselves these two questions:

1. What is the worst thing that can happen if I make this move?
2. How will I handle this worst-case scenario?

Once the person doing this exercise has asked, confronted, and answered these two questions, his fears are cut down to manageable size and his confidence grows, for he now knows exactly how to handle the very worst thing that can happen. For instance, your son may pose this question to himself: "What is the worst thing that can happen if I take this job that I'm not sure of?" Well, the job could turn out to be unredeemably awful. Your son could go on to ask how that worst case could be dealt with.

The answer would be that he could resign and get another job. Or he could start his own business, if he concludes that the job is awful because he hates to work for anybody except the most understanding boss in the world, himself.

Try the worst-case scenario exercise. It's very useful.

One last obstacle in the launching of children, according to parents, is the unrealistic expectations their offspring have about the work world. They feel their kids have cock-eyed ideas such as:

It is easy to get to the top.

I will get promotions and money because I am "hot stuff."

I will be able to afford to live as my parents do on my salary.

This last notion drives parents crazy. As one mother said, "They have no idea about the relationship between effort and material things. They just don't translate the sweat at work into what things cost at stores."

Often only experience can correct these attitudes. Our kids will find out what we have found out—that it isn't easy to get to the top, or even just inside the door.

This chapter has covered some of the overall issues and specific parent experiences connected to emptying the nest. In the next chapter, we'll turn to what happens when a young adult returns home to live. Never mind the fact that in high school the only way to get and keep them home was to let the air out of their tires. That was then, this is now, and you need to know what to do when Tammy or Tommy turns up on your doorstep.

2

Living at Home

Home Sweet Home Again

Pushed by the high cost of living and the need for a safe and friendly harbor, grown-up kids are returning home. This remigration was reported by about half the families I surveyed, which represents just a fraction of the millions of parents in the country who find their kids back home in their bunkbeds once more. So it's parenthood, stage two, in the United States: The kids come home, wagging their tails behind them. Or, perhaps, they just test the waters to see how their parents feel about their coming back for a while.

And how do you feel? If you're like some parents, you may feel confused. Yes, you'd like to help out, but you're

27

enjoying your own life these days. Or, yes, it would be nice to lend them a hand as they get started, but are you keeping them dependent by letting them stay at home?

This last concern—dependency—seems to be a key part of our thinking about what it means to be a grown-up in twentieth-century America. Whereas many other cultures place a value on keeping the clan together—if not in the same house or block, at least in the same town—we do not. We've been taught that "real" grown-ups leave home and move away to follow jobs or mates. This separation from the family is so ingrained in our thinking that kids who live at home after the school years have to explain themselves to their judgmental peers: "Well, it's just until I get some money together." Or, "It's just until I find a job." And parents who "allow" kids to return home for a while feel slightly uneasy sometimes. Are they doing something wrong?

Now, you'd expect a book on the subject of launching kids to advise getting the youngsters out of the house and keeping them out of the house—period—but that's not what you'll read here. Having the kids make a postcollege pit stop (my daughter's term) can be a pleasure and a help all around. The young ones get an economic breather and some good companionship as they start out and you get what you've worked toward for twenty years: a chance to enjoy the very nice young adult you've brought up.

However, a live-in arrangement with a child is much like marriage. It works very well for some people and not at all well for others. For instance, if you have spent several decades fighting with one of your offspring and you just don't get along, then you are not, in my opinion, a good candidate for a live-in situation. But if, in general, you've gotten along with just occasional minor skirmishes, you may enjoy having a kid back home, at least for a while.

The Nitty-Gritty

Since the success of living together often depends on how the daily nitty-gritty is handled, this section will offer specific pointers on how to navigate some common concerns. Let's begin at the beginning. That's when you first discuss their returning home. . . .

COME TO AN AGREEMENT ABOUT THE LENGTH OF THE STAY

Although you do not have to pinpoint the exact date of departure, it's sensible to agree on the nature of the stay. It may be until an offspring gets a job, usually a matter of some months. Or it may be until she saves enough for a down payment on a house or a deposit on an apartment. Or you both may like to leave it open-ended, as in, "Okay, we'll do this as long as it feels right." Often, the arrival of a strong love interest in the life of your offspring will be the point at which it doesn't feel right to live at home any longer.

Agreeing on expectations will prevent hurt feelings and misunderstandings later. After all, if a daughter feels free to stay as long as she wants, but your unvoiced expectation is that she will find another place as soon as she finds a job, then you have set yourselves up for unpleasantness. My offspring have stayed anywhere from six weeks to two years, and all of the various schedules worked out well.

(During this postcollege live-at-home phase, whatever length it is, you may find children over twenty much more fun than children in the full heat of rebellion, say fifteen or sixteen. In fact, I would suggest that it become the societal norm to ship them out of the house in their midteens to a location undisclosed even unto you, and to have them at home in their young adulthood, when they are, in many ways, a delight.)

AGREE ON HOW TO HANDLE THE "PULL-APARTS" OF LIVING TOGETHER

By pull-aparts, I mean the supposedly small things that drive housemates to distraction: smoking, loud music, late parties, not showing up for meals, sexual sleep-overs, someone taking the milk you were saving for your coffee, undone dishes, unmade beds, unfed pets, wilted houseplants, dust balls, too many drinks, drug use and abuse, and on and on and on. Given the richness and diversity of possible disagreements, it's a wonder that we can live with anyone besides ourselves.

Now, many of these issues have probably already been resolved, because this is no stranger living in your house. This is a child you have known intimately. But if there are new issues, sexual sleep-overs, for instance, or unresolved old issues, perhaps smoking or drug use, then now may be the time to get them discussed and resolved.

Our solution for the one smoker in our family was that he smoke outside, no exceptions—rain, wind, or tornado. I spent too much time and energy overcoming the habit myself to tolerate more smoke in my life. I'm a real hard-liner on this issue and would have a kid move away before I would let him or her induce lung cancer and respiratory disease in the rest of us through indoor secondhand smoke.

You probably have one or two things you may be a hard-liner about. If so, settle the issue up front or you'll encounter trouble later. For many parents, it's drugs. If your kid won't say no and it drives you crazy, then living at home won't work. At all. So *you* say no.

And forget the notion of reforming the young person. Some parents take in their kids with the idea of getting them off chemical dependencies, perhaps alcohol or cocaine. It most likely will not work. Leave it to the professional drug and alcohol rehab centers or to AA to help. (If drugs or alcohol are a problem close to home, see chapter 5.)

Another potential source of friction is differing house-keeping standards, an infamous pull-apart for people trying to live together. If one of you is a neatnik and the other a beatnik, consider a common area/private area approach. Each one picks up after herself in the common areas—living room, kitchen, and so on—but each person's bedroom is her kingdom. Clothes can be thrown, beds never made. Just keep the bedroom door shut so the rest of the family doesn't have to see it.

Music is another thing that drives parents crazy, both in kind and volume. Acid rock at top decibel is not a fifty-year-old's favorite sound. A portable tape player/radio with ear phones is a great peacemaker here. These devices injure only their eardrums, not yours.

If you can't agree on TV shows, get two sets.

If you can't agree on foods, each can cook her own. Separatist cuisine. Or let whoever cooks for the family call the shots on the menu. We combined the two approaches. Each person handled her own breakfast and lunch. Then we traded off cooking dinners, with the cook in charge of the menu. And sometimes we cooked together, one person doing the main course and the other the veggies and salad.

People who aren't going to show up for dinner should call ahead and let the cook know.

RESPECT YOUR OWN FEELINGS ON THE SEX PARTNER/SLEEP-OVER ISSUE

There is a huge spectrum of reaction when it comes to off-spring having a two-person pajama party at the parents' house. Some families would never allow it. Sex outside marriage just seems wrong, especially under a parental roof. Other families are a little uncomfortable, but kind of look the other way. After all, they think, times have changed. Still others are very relaxed and think it's only natural that their children's loved ones be included in the household. If that means staying over sometimes, so be it. One mother even complained to me that she wished her daughter and her boyfriend would stop staying at a nearby hotel during visits to mom and dad and stay with the family instead. This mother felt that if everybody stayed under one roof, it would mean more visiting time.

You have to find your own way on this. If there's a continuing argument within the family, it's time for your young person to seek other quarters. You don't need to spend your middle age in a no-win struggle over sexual mores.

Interestingly, the shoe can sometimes be on the other foot. Sometimes, single parents wonder if it's okay to bring their lovers home for an overnight. What will the children think? Well, again, it is a private call. Just don't ask your kids to practice celibacy at home while you cavort in front of them. That's a double standard and will make you no friends on the home front.

AGREE ON HOUSEHOLD RESPONSIBILITIES AND ENFORCE THEM

Put this one in the easier-said-than-done category. It's easy to agree, but hard, in the press of life, to keep agreements. I personally hate the enforcer role and its nagging rhetoric: "Georgie, it's your turn to vacuum."

My solution is to have a janitorial service come in once a week to dredge the place out. It's a luxury, of course, but I would do without new clothes or vacations before I would do without a cleaning service. It not only saves a lot of time and energy but it saves arguing over whose turn it is to clean the johns. Anyhow, is it a major goal of your life to be known as a marvy housekeeper? I have never wanted to have it said during my funeral service that I was known for the relentless pursuit of the American dust ball. If you feel the same and can swing it, get help.

If you hate housekeeping but can't afford help—no way, no how—don't let yourself get stuck as the only house-keeper. You're all roommates in this enterprise and every-body should pitch in. If you need to make a weekly schedule of who does what, write it and post it on the refrigerator door and keep people to it. Go on strike if they don't keep up their end of the deal. Or, kick 'em out. You don't need to spend midlife as a scullery maid. Those years are over.

There is one chore, though, that you will never be able to get your kids to do, so give up now. That is replacing a roll of toilet paper. In thirty years, no child of mine has ever replaced a paper roll. They think it's done by the bath-room fairy. Or perhaps something is wrong with their manual dexterity that this humble activity is beyond them. At any rate, I hope you succeed in this noble enterprise—getting them paper-trained, so to speak—but I, who have gone before you, have failed.

MIND YOUR OWN BUSINESS, AT LEAST MOST OF THE TIME

It's hard to keep your nose out of the affairs of people you love, but when I'm tempted to intervene inappropriately, I remember dear Mother Saint Helen, my fifth-grade teacher. She taught me one thing that year: MYOB, which means *mind your own business.*

Golden words, they are, and I have tried to MYOB all the years since. Now, it's easy to keep from telling Margaret Thatcher what she should do in England, and it's easy to keep from telling the president what to do about the budget, but it's not easy to keep from telling your daughter what you think of her haircuts, her friends, her clothes, her music, and her current patois, whatever it is—valley girl, beat, and so on.

And she has the same problem with you.

So my kids and I have made a pact. We swear that we will not interfere with each other's lives unless we see the other about to fall off a cliff. If we see one of us about to make a very serious misstep, we speak up. We don't nag; we don't keep at it until the other does what we want. We just make our case diplomatically and then, having voiced our concerns, we try and shut up and leave the subject alone.

It works pretty well, because we don't interfere with each other on a day-to-day basis and we feel secure in the knowledge that the rest of the pack will say something if one of us is about to step off a metaphorical cliff—or a real one, for that matter.

EXPECT A CONTRIBUTION

There should be some effort forthcoming from the younger generation, some way of kicking in resources toward the common good of the household. It can be money—room and board, for instance—or it can be services of any kind. They can run errands, for instance.

Here are some errands that our live-at-homes have done to help out: take the TV set in for repairs, do the food shopping, pick up the clothes at the dry cleaners, cut the wood, change the oil in the car, make breakfast/lunch/dinner, move furniture, wash cars, weed the back forty, wash the dog, plant the vegetable bed, trim the trees, bring the car in for repairs, fix the scarecrow, harvest grapes, fertilize the garden, fix the TV antenna, set up the new stereo, do the dishes, decorate the Christmas tree, wrap presents, start fires, make wine, take the dog to the vet, put out snail bait, make flower arrangements, replace a front door—and that's just part of it. The fact is, offspring have many, many ways to contribute.

Let them know their work is valued and make sure the lazy ones contribute, too. I think it erodes self-esteem to allow kids to live in and not contribute. It sure doesn't prepare them for life. On some level, they lose respect for themselves for behaving like boors, and on another level, they probably lose some respect for you for letting them get away with such behavior.

TRY AND AGREE WITH YOUR SPOUSE/ PARTNER ABOUT THE MAIN ISSUES CONNECTED WITH A LIVE-IN KID, ESPECIALLY WITH THE BASIC ONE: DO YOU BOTH WANT TO DO THIS AT ALL?

If you found it difficult to agree on child-related issues before, you will most likely still disagree. If you usually agree, you're lucky. The point is, one of you alone shouldn't negotiate and make deals and agreements on a live-in situation that involves the two of you. You're in it together. If you attempt a live-in situation with one of you clearly against it, resentment will build. Household human relations will be strained and negative.

Sometimes a compromise can be worked out such as:

Wife to husband: "I know you're not keen on having Jimmy here. You think he should have a place of his own. And that's what he'd like eventually, too. But would you consider his living with us until he makes enough money for first and last month's rent on an apartment?"

Sometimes these compromises will work, especially if the length of the stay has a time limit. And sometimes they won't work, because nothing in a relationship works when a situation is foisted on an unwilling participant. Unwillingness will show itself, often in the form of short tempers or fault-finding.

Another solution when parents aren't keen on the prodigal's return is to lend or give that all-important first and last month's rent to get the offspring off the launching pad. If it's a loan, insist that it be repaid in the agreed-upon time.

THE SUCCESS OF A LIVE-IN ARRANGEMENT WILL OFTEN DEPEND ON THE DEGREE OF PRIVACY AFFORDED TO BOTH GENERATIONS

If you have a garage, attic, or playroom that can be converted into the live-in's den or lair, all of you will benefit. You won't get in each other's hair so much. I'm convinced that live-in arrangements worked well for our family because we had one bedroom and bath completely away from the main traffic of the house, plus a room off the garage with its own entrance.

Because houses and apartments seem to get smaller and smaller as rents and mortgages get larger and larger, privacy is more difficult to find than ever before. If you are living in a small house or apartment, it will be hard to find enough space so each generation will have turf unto itself. Just do the best you can.

One outlet that helps when tempers get short is a daily workout at the gym. Somehow gyms can turn into a home away from home for young people—a place to exercise, shower, be with peers. I don't know how or why it works, but exercise, even just a neighborhood walk, seems to make home life sweet when it's beginning to taste a little stale or sour. If you really want to sweeten up the atmosphere, go to the gym or exercise yourself. It's hard to worry or be resentful when you're panting through an aerobics routine.

One last observation on living quarters: You are in for a surprise if you haven't shared a bathroom with a live-in offspring for a while. Gone are the days when all that adorned a bathroom was a bottle of Prell, a cake of Ivory soap, a jar of Pond's cold cream, and a toothbrush. Be prepared for a crowded medicine cabinet and jammed-up shelves. You'll find renewer creams and stress creams—one formulation for the face and another for the eyes. And there are cuticle nourishers—do you want your daughter to have undernourished cuticles?—and ridge-filling base coats for the nails, along with conditioners that flaunt nucleic acids and electrolytes. And then there'll be natural cosmetics taking up your shelf space—those bottles and jars full of aloe, lecithin, avocado, cucumber, and goat's milk. Do not show your age and ignorance by eating this stuff. It goes on the outside of you. And remember that the kids hide the really expensive shampoos and conditioners under the sink.

Conclusions, Or What I Learned as an Advanced Den Mother

Almost every parent I have ever talked with expressed a worry about making their kids dependent by giving them a roof for a while. Relax. Independence is not necessarily a matter of geography, of *where* one lives in relation to other members of the family. Your kids are not going to be hopelessly dependent just because they live at home for a stretch any more than they are going to be independent because they live "away." All four of my offspring lived at home postcollege and each has migrated satisfactorily into adulthood.

I asked one parent of a large brood how it had worked for her and her husband to have their kids home for a while after college. Had it interfered with their growing up? She told me that she thought living at home had actually given the kids a head start on adulthood: "Jim, my husband, has done well in the computer business and several of the kids wanted to go into the same business. They really picked his brain about the business. When they were teenagers, of course, they weren't interested, but later, in their twenties, they not only wanted the benefit of his experience but they asked for it. He was able to give them a leg up on getting started. Not that he got them jobs, though he did give them leads. No, he really just gave them an insider's view of how the business worked. I think it gave the kids a competitive edge. Believe me, they didn't turn out dependent. Neither Jim nor I could stomach that. We didn't raise them to be clinging vines."

According to sociologist Allan Schnaiberg, who has studied the launching of young adults, there are at least two good questions to ask yourself about your kids living at home: (1) Does the arrangement help them progress in some way toward maturity? (2) Are you giving them the consistent message that you expect them to grow toward independence? If the arrangement measures up to these two criteria, it may be a good one.

Now, if you think independence is just a matter of geography—that is, where one lives—consider the people you know who live away from home but call constantly for guidance, opinions, direction, and general shoring up. Are they more independent than an offspring who lives at home for a while after college, but who pretty much controls her own life? Not in my mind. Independence is as independence does.

I'd like to share what it's taken me over fifty years to learn about independence. Like many other things in life, independence can be overdone, overrated, and overused. The American ideal of the independent loner—strong, stoic, looking only within for emotional sustenance and support—can be dangerous.

It seems to me much more safe and sane to have robust links to family, spouse, friends, and neighbors. This network makes one stronger, not weaker. Many sources of support are far more reliable than depending only on oneself. I fear for the loner, because his well-being depends so heavily on his relationship with one person—himself. It's healthy to seek companionship and support. And in bad times, to share sorrow and troubles with other humans is not weak but essential, a strengthening use of interdependence and friendship. Maybe the word *depend* should get taken out of the junk pile and put right up there with other warm and fuzzy words such as love and kindness.

Of course, any of these—love, kindness, interdependence—can get us into trouble when taken to an extreme. Just think of kids who are crippled by parental kindness and people who are so dependent on others that they have no inner self to rely on. My conclusion about these issues is that the Greeks had it figured out a long time ago: the Golden Mean—in other words, balance. Not too much, not too little. It comes down to this incongruity: Stand on your own two feet, but lean on others for support. Don't worry if you're giving a helping hand to your offspring for a while. Just don't overhelp. Anyway, you won't be doing it when they're forty. In fact, by then it may be the other way around: *they* may be helping *you*.

Baby, Cookie Mom, and Plaid Dad

In my life as den mother to young adults I've also learned that the rules about playing mommy, daddy, and baby change. In fact, there should be no baby role when a young adult comes home. Baby is lost and gone forever, that is, unless you want to spend your middle years wet-nursing an overgrown child.

You are now dealing with a young adult who may be living with you, but who is capable of earning her own living, making decisions, and, wonder of wonders, learning to work the washing machine, the dryer, the dishwasher, the vacuum cleaner, and the microwave. (You already know that she can operate the videotape recorder better than you. This is normal. Whenever your kids, especially your male kids, protest that they can't learn to use the oven, remember that you are getting stonewalled. Anybody who can watch one TV program and tape another, while making audio tapes of your compact discs, can learn to turn on an oven.)

The idea of baby and the behavior of baby should get packed away along with the notion of an all-present, all-loving cookie mom and the fantasy of the perfect father who always lends his car and wears a plaid shirt. I call him the plaid dad.

41

Cookie mom and plaid dad are dreams that many kids cling to. I had these illusions when I was little. For me, cookie mom was the mother in the Dick and Jane readers. She had on a freshly pressed gingham house dress with an apron over it, and, in my imaginings, she always had a plate of cookies fresh from the oven to counteract the rigors of the first grade.

Cookie moms, at least in our yearnings, also make great mashed potatoes and beaten biscuits. They can use iodine on cut knees without it stinging, comb hair without it hurting, and are always there, usually in the kitchen, but sometimes in the garden. Cookie moms, in other words, are perfect. When we are little, we all want one. When we are big, we of the female persuasion all aspire in our hearts to be cookie moms, at least some of the time.

As for plaid dads, they are another fantasy, a dream of a wise, all-knowing father, smoking a pipe in his tartan shirts, a backyard saint in chinos. In our imaginations, he dispensed love and wisdom, but never anything as gross as an actual spanking.

Alas, there are no cookie moms and plaid dads. Just us perfectly normal imperfect parents. So if you haven't yet put aside the fanatasy of yourself as the perfect parent, now is the time to do it. You are not the Huxtables. You are not Lassie's mom or dad. You are probably an overworked, overconfused, and pretty nice parent who cares about the kids you've brought up. Why else would you be reading this book?

If you are still taking elaborate care of the needs of your offspring, consider cutting it out and doing something else with your energy. This kind of service is a disservice to your kids, especially as far as getting the respect of their peers.

There is a mysterious tom-tom system among young people: They sense what friends are being babied by parents and they scorn them. I know one bachelor in his thirties who lives in San Francisco. He's been enormously successful in a high-technology business, yet the young ladies about town giggle at him. They've told me, "His mother still does his laundry. Who could get serious about him?" Think of that the next time you're tempted to play laundress with your offspring.

Now, it's easy to say let's all be adult, but it's hard sometimes to translate this ideal into action. Who hasn't stumbled over the issue of how to treat our newly fledged adults as adults?

One way of fostering adulthood is doing what you've been doing for years: transferring responsibility for their lives from you to them. They are the ones in charge now. It doesn't mean you can't lend a hand. It doesn't mean they can't ask for advice. It does mean that they are the owners of their lives.

Think of it this way. When kids are born, they are the minority shareholders of their own lives. You and your spouse are president and CEO of this new enterprise known as your child. Gradually, other people come onto the board of directors: teachers, grandparents, and in the teen years, peers and media role models. But precollege young people are still not the chief executive officers of their own lives. It is only when they start earning their own livings, picking their own friends and lovers, deciding on the use of their own time that they become true managers of themselves. As they matured, you, if you were wise, were handing over the reins to them, giving them authority equal to the responsibility they were willing to shoulder. If these two things, authority and responsibility, are kept equal, many home problems get solved.

For example, your daughter may hate how you organize your kitchen, but if she takes no responsibility for cooking, she should have no authority in the matter. Authority should be equal to responsibility. It's a law that settles many a family dispute over who should call the shots on an issue.

Let's leave the subject of family roles within the household to take a look at what other parents say about their experiences with live-in kids. . . .

What Other Parents Say

As noted before, about half of the people in my survey had postcollege kids live with them. These live-in periods ranged from six weeks to three years, with most falling within the three- to eighteen-month range. Parents said their kids came home for economic reasons, for mutual companionship and support, and just because there was room.

Contrary to the myth, which can be summed up as "What a drag!" these families reported an overwhelmingly positive experience. It wasn't a drag for them: They enjoyed it. The rewards far outweighed the drawbacks.

Listen to what they had to say about their kids' return home:

"I got to experience my fun-loving daughter on a daily basis."

"We enjoyed his company, as did his younger sisters."

"It was wonderful. We had sent a kid to college and got back this extraordinarily humorous, kind, handsome conversationalist and he and his brother—eight years younger—became best friends. It was one of the most splendid two years we ever had."

So much for the myth that the experience has to be negative.

Basically, the rewards for the parents were several. Companionship, especially the discovery of their offspring as a nice adult, was mentioned frequently:

"We learned how to lean on each other and gained a great deal from living as two adult women together, rather than as mother and daughter."

"It was a chance to know them as adults and to discuss many things that were not pertinent to a high school or college kid, that is, how business and life really work."

Other parents spoke of the pleasure of getting to know the young person without siblings around:

"We finally got to know him on a one-to-one basis, since all the other kids were gone."

"She has us to herself and we have her to ourselves."

Still others appreciated having another pair of hands in the house and yard:

"He's fun, chops wood, and walks the dog."

"We ate well. She's an excellent cook."

"We have a built-in house-sitter."

"She babysits with the younger kids when I'm away on business trips."

Emotional support, from child to parent, was mentioned frequently:

"She was a companion during an unusual family illness."

"Provided emotional support for us during trying times with elderly parents."

Parents enjoyed lending a hand during the crucial passage to adulthood:

"I got real satisfaction by helping emotionally and practically. We were both looking for a job at the same time, so we traded information about the businesses in the area, salaries, etc."

Some parents got into the live-in business through misfortune: Their kids were recovering from a serious accident or illness:

"He came to recover from a life-threatening accident. He stayed a while after he recuperated, which was fine with us."

Another mother nursed her son through a disabling on-the-job accident. Her son also stayed on because the arrangement turned out to be one they all liked.

Now, was the experience of parents all positive? Of course not, though about 15 percent of the parents did say there were no drawbacks at all to the arrangement:

"My husband and I used to sit and look at each other and try to figure out why we were so lucky."

But most parents, when specifically asked, did mention some drawbacks. More work for the lady of the house was one of the reservations mentioned most frequently.

"Too much work for a working mom."

"I bear the brunt of the extra work which I have little time for."

Related to that was another problem, lack of clarity about who is responsible for what around the house:

"Resolving household responsibilities was difficult."

Lack of consideration was also sometimes a negative.

"I'd like to know how many to expect for dinner."

46

"I had to train him to write us a note when he used up the last of any household supply or food."

Other parents, especially single moms whose income had been eaten into by divorce, mentioned money as a problem.

"I can't afford the utilities. When kids are here, I need financial help."

"My son owes me $75 a month for several months of phone bills."

Another concern was space, either lacking it or having the kids not respect the parent's space and privacy. (Anybody who has had a drawer rifled or makeup and clothes borrowed and never returned will know what an irritation that can be.)

Last, one divorced mother with a spirited sense of humor told me that the biggest drawback she had was "brain damage, from doing it alone." She also told me that she solved her problems with her two adult daughters by moving out herself to live with her boyfriend—an unusual but highly creative solution.

With kids at home, how did parents resolve difficulties between the generations? By and large, the parents talked it out with their offspring. Honest negotiations were the order of the day, though some admitted to an occasional yelling match. One mother said, "Sometimes we just agreed to disagree and argue. Other times we said, " 'This isn't worth it. I really love you too much to act like this.' " There were no magic solutions to conflict. Families just talked it over.

One father encapsulated the situation nicely: "This is a time of renegotiation—of renegotiating how you will live together, but this time as adults."

A therapist interviewed said she thought it was far easier to work things out with postcollege kids than with teen-agers, for many of the problems of rebellion and defiance disappear with maturity.

When asked if they were criticized by family or friends for having kids live at home, most parents answered no. The ones who answered yes mentioned that often other family members, especially siblings, did the criticizing. Was this the jealousy of sibling rivalry in action? I don't know the answer, but the question should be asked by any parent who's getting flak from her other kids.

There were some surprising answers to the question about criticism. Several parents said not only weren't they criticized but they were envied:

"It was obvious we were enjoying ourselves. We might have been subject more to envy than criticism."

"I think we were envied rather then criticized, because our child was willing to stay at home and share the burden [of a grandmother's illness] rather than larking off on her own."

Parents seemed to let criticism roll off their backs. Not one said it made any difference in their behavior. It was an irritant, but not a determining factor in how they lived their lives.

To sum up the experience of these parents, most found the experience of having a live-in offspring a positive one. They enjoyed the companionship, had fun, and appreciated the help. The downside was extra work for mom, some lack of consideration on the part of the kids, a little crowding, and some worry about the extra bills. Most families handled their conflicts by talking them out.

The Single Parent

For the single parent, a live-in offspring presents a slightly different operating framework. The single parent does not have the support of another seasoned adult in the house. All battles must be fought alone. Often, too, the decision making, the hard thinking, must be done solo. (Why don't people acknowledge that parenting is hefty cerebral exercise? Bringing up young people requires a lot of thought. My brain certainly runs overtime trying to figure out what to do, what to say, how to guide, when not to guide, and so on.)

The single parent does most of the doing and thinking alone and is, for better or worse, the captain of the household ship. There are advantages to being captain. You don't have to consult a cocaptain. No partner is present to throw out a dissenting viewpoint. Nobody vetoes your decision on the ground rules. You're on your own, which can translate into a real mixed bag: lonely but with a clear and certain authority, free to set the rules of the house.

But, if you want to talk something over and are lucky enough to have a reasonable and intelligent ex-spouse, you can pick up the phone. This also helps the ex-spouse, for he or she can still be connected in a useful way to the lives of the children. Too often, men, especially, are exiled by divorce from involvement with their children. Oh, yes, they have the dutiful visits, the shared meal out, the ritual how-are-you's, but sometimes the only meaningful contribution they are asked to make is with their wallets. So, if you have a well-meaning ex-spouse, you may wish to pick up the phone and solicit another viewpoint about whether or not young Jim should be going to grad school or working so hard or loafing so much or seeing a shrink or taking a year off to bum around the world.

Of course, the single parent gets one great benefit when a young person comes home for a while, and that's daily companionship. When the two people involved are compatible, and the ground rules are set so that each fully respects the other's independence and privacy, a living together arrangement can work out well.

Case in point: I was a single parent living alone in the family house. My eldest son had started his first job. Rents in the area were high, so we said, why not cast in our lots together for a while? He came home and took up residence in a semiseparate part of the house. He paid room and board, less than he would have paid in the "real" world, but enough to help me out with the expenses of running the house. Both of us got economic relief and a friendly face at the end of the day. He was free to come and go when he wanted. Me, too. Often, he would go off for the weekend with friends. I would do the same.

What I remember from those years are the great conversations on weekday nights over dinner. Both of us were in the beginning stages of trying to understand the business world. He was learning the nitty-gritty that he hadn't learned as an economics major in college, and I was learning what I hadn't learned as that most naive of creatures, a housewife.

It was fun, satisfying, and great to know him as an adult. He eventually found more private quarters, which was fine with me. Things flow, change, and grow. And his time at home evidently didn't hinder his independence. He runs his own successful business, has a wonderful wife, and directs his own life.

Actually, all four of my kids have lived at home postcollege, along with three live-in loaners. (This is what happens when you have empty bedrooms.) One young man was with us for more than a year, paying his room and board faithfully, and helping me renovate part of the house. He was a fine housemate and I'd do it again. Only later did I learn that anthropologists call this "aunting," which is being a semimom to someone else's offspring, who are more or less on loan for a while.

Aunting is not at all a bad idea, especially if you are single, have an empty house, and like the company. Other people's kids will behave better for you than they do for their parents, and yours will behave better at someone else's house than they do at yours. Ironically, this young man's mother was aunting herself, providing a home for still another young person. And so the nurturing got passed on, family to family.

Once I learned the concept of aunting, I began spotting the phenomenon all over the place. My parents, when I left for college, had a young French girl from the Experiment in International Living stay with them for a year. That was aunting. A writer friend of mine had a home that always sheltered at least one nonrelated young person. More aunting. You can probably think of some aunting examples yourself.

A Few More Tips

Here are some additional ways to weight things in favor of success.

The arrangement can work much better if the live-in

has a job. Gone are the tensions that come from job hunting, job rejections, no money, and no place to go in the
morning. Things are simply more relaxed when the young
one is working and out of the house all day. But you can't
make a job magically appear. You are not a personnel office:
You're a parent. You can, though, give support and a little
coaching. Remember that the next chapter, "Getting the
First Job," is there to help you help them through the job-
hunting process.

On your side, it is also useful if you are significantly
involved with your own interests. Parenting may be rewarding, but, full-time, it's not a fit occupation for a forty- or
fifty-year-old. This book and its tips are meant to fill the
spaces around the edge of your life, not be the main text.

So try to make sure that both parents and kids have
several sources of satisfaction in life. No one person in the
arrangement should be the sole lifeline of the other. All,
ideally, should be active with family, friends, love partners,
work—both paid and volunteer—hobbies, and other interests. The sources of support should have many branches.
That way, if one support fails, the others are in place.

Now, be a romantic for a minute here and think of
your life as a tapestry in the making. There are many colors
and strands, all going to make up the individual wonderment
called your life. You may be about half-finished with this
work of art as you read this. You'll be weaving the strands
for perhaps another thirty or forty years. There's more
designing to do, much more life pattern to work out. As you
weave, try to keep the perspective of the whole. Having a
child at home for a while can be a pleasant and sunny motif
in the design, but not the whole.

And yet, at the same time, in a mystifying irony, our

children will occupy our hearts for as long as we live, wherever they live. As a mother in Marilyn French's novel, *Her Mother's Daughter*, says about her children:

> I adore them. I would not be without them. Then and now: I still . . . what can I call it? Not love. More than love and not excluding hate. My heart is tied to them with unbreakable cord. The cord is scarred, pulled thin, has been hacked at, but it does not break. It is a towrope stronger than what it is attached to, strong enough to rip apart the heart before it breaks.

And that is why we savor the short time we have with these new young adults.

3

Getting the First Job

How Parents Can Lend a Hand

There are, I am told, young people who major in relevant and useful subjects, who work each summer during college at jobs that are "going somewhere," who know exactly what they want to be when they grow up and have job offers waiting for them by April of their senior year in college. Mind you, I've never met such a creature, but I'm told they exist.

You may have never met such a creature either, let alone have one as a child. And if you, like many other parents, brought up your kids without pressure, a mode

54

greatly favored in the sixties and seventies, if you were reluctant to push them too hard, it's no wonder that they may now be adrift occupationally rather than focused tightly on a profession. So join the ranks of parents who need to learn a few things about job hunting to pass on to the next generation.

But first, let's ask this question: What are we doing in the job-hunting business anyhow? PTA, school sports, dance chaperones—those are the normal things parents sign up for when they produce little ones, but nobody told us in the delivery room that we were going to have to help find this seven-pound baby a job in twenty-one years.

Just what are we doing as career counselor or placement officer? Isn't it somebody's else's job? For instance, how about the schools? The colleges? Or what about a government job placement agency?

The fact is, nobody else is doing much to help your family member get a job. Though some colleges have excellent career centers, the parents I heard from said the career counseling they encountered was either "spotty," terrible, or nonexistent (more later about how to evaluate a college career center).

School counselors are often overwhelmed by too heavy a load of students. Some have not kept up-to-date on the job market. And government job agencies don't offer a lot in the way of attractive job listings, because many employers don't and won't list jobs with them. Employers want qualified people who already have jobs, not the desperately out-of-work. (Don't look at me. I didn't make the rules.)

To make matters worse, job-hunting skills are often neglected in the school curriculum. How often have you seen courses such as Job Hunting 101? Some exist, but my family spies tell me they can be dull courses taught by instructors whose knowledge of the subject stems from theory rather than real life.

Like it or not, then, the chore of helping with the job hunt falls partly, at least, on the family. Most of us are not prepared for it. Helping kids find their professional place in the world just hasn't been part of our parenting education or practice. Perhaps it's because the rules about job finding change all the time, so there's been no consistent body of knowledge for parents to receive and pass on. For instance, in one decade the world needs teachers, but in the next decade there's a glut of teachers. Or in one decade engineers are needed and then there's a glut of engineers. Such instability in supply and demand is likely to make advice-giving parents feel as though they might be giving yesterday's advice to today's kids. Well-meaning irrelevancy is what we bewildered and slightly out-of-date parents often pass on as home-grown job counseling.

But you *can* help, even as the work world changes. If you have kids who would appreciate a little unobtrusive coaching from a very interested friend—you—you can pick up some basics here to pass on. Better that than being a well-wisher on the sidelines.

Please note, though, that I am not suggesting taking over the job hunt. There are parents who overhelp. They make phone calls to employers on behalf of their kids, pressure people who owe them favors to hire Jason or Stacey, and go overboard throwing around their weight and opinions. This behavior diminishes the participation of the young person, whose role is reduced to putting on a suit and going in for the job interview.

Helping your child get a job is a delicate operation, like

teaching him to ride a two-wheel bike. It won't work with you in the cyclist's seat and him perched on back. Instead, he should get his own chance in the driver's seat. You can run beside him, lending support until he gets the hang of it.

And then you let go.

Let's take a look at fantasy versus reality when it comes to a job hunt. This section is designed to prepare you for reality, so you won't think you're alone when your offspring sweat over their resumes, cry over their rejections, and either freeze up or talk too much during their job interviews.

A FAIRY-TALE JOB HUNT

Once upon a time there was a young collegian, who decided on her life's work at the end of her sophomore year. This was just in time to choose a perfect major, which not only prepared her in useful detail for her prospective career but provided her with a broad, meaningful liberal arts education. Every summer during college, this young woman worked at a paid internship that prepared her to enter her career at the speed of light.

At the end of her junior year, our heroine methodically read every good book on careers and job hunting, all the while beginning to cultivate an extensive network of friends and professional acquaintances to assist her in her eventual job hunt.

By March of her senior year, she mailed beautifully composed letters of application along with a dazzling and flawless resume that stopped personnel officers in their tracks. Interviews were sought and granted.

By April, our heroine was interviewed by the finest of companies. Her pantyhose only ran once and of course she had a replacement pair in the glove compartment of her car. Her smile and hair spray never failed.

In May, she was offered and accepted a fine job. The job was exciting and challenging. It involved no typing, grunt work, or late hours. The salary was more than enough to accommodate a charming little starter home and the beginnings of a large bank account.

After graduation in June, as our heroine moved her belongings from the family home, she said to her mother and father:

"Oh, dearest parents, how I hate to leave, but I must. Everything I've done and everything I am today, I owe to you. From now on, I will be financially independent, bringing you only joy and pride in the years to come."

And then our heroine walks off into the sunset, thoughtfully clearing her room of her old yearbooks, stuffed animals, and withered corsages from high school proms. Her job, of course, will be divine. Her company will suffer no mergers or layoffs, her career path no obstacles, her stomach no ulcers.

And that is how it is supposed to be in the best of all possible worlds. But here's how it often really is . . . .

A TRUE-TO-LIFE STORY

This particular heroine isn't sure what she'd like to major in, because it is difficult to tell what will most become the next Christie Brinkley or Madonna. Confused, she switches her major from fashion merchandising to theater arts, but needs to take a fifth year of college because the theater arts courses are all filled up and the college refuses to put in more sections. She writes home, "Sorry about another year's tuition, but, I mean, you *know* how totally stupid colleges can be."

One month after graduation, our heroine realizes that there is more to life than hanging out with her boyfriend and doing her nails. The task, as she sees it, is that a girl needs some bread, because there are great fall clothes to buy and it's a drag living with these two older people (they claim to be her parents) who keep shoving the help-wanted pages under her nose first thing every morning at 11 A.M.

Pressured into motion, something happens with our heroine. It is not quite a job hunt. More a job saunter, a meandering through possibilities. One company is contacted through the want ads. One neighbor tells of a secretarial opening in his office. A girlfriend invites our heroine to become famous together in New York.

The parents suggest she instead become famous locally as an employed person. They help write a resume. They help write: strong people skills, flexible, good communicator. They want to write: personal interests—tanning, doing nails, dieting, drinking wine coolers, the pecs and abs of the male body.

Autumn falls and our heroine takes a waitressing job to keep body and wardrobe together. Six months of that are enough. She misses her former theater interests. She goes to New York. She waitresses there while she auditions. Six months of that are enough. She comes back home, humbled and weary, learning at last that it takes more than a perfect coat of Misty Pearl nail polish to assure professional success.

Our heroine then returns to an old love, fashion. She gets a job at the local department store. She sells clothes like mad. She gets promoted. She loves her job. She gets promoted more. She works hard. She has found, if not all of herself, at least a very comfortable part that is successful.

It took a few years. It took several false starts. She read no job-hunting books. She went to no counselor, took no aptitude tests, did little networking. In short, she stumbled along and fell, willy-nilly, into some niche that felt right for her.

And that's real life.

In fact, in a recent Gallup poll, only 41 percent of the employed respondents said they consciously chose their job or career. Most people said they got started by chance or took the only job available. Sixty-five percent, regretting the hit-and-miss way they got jobs, said that given the chance to start over, they would try to get more information about career choices. Pass that statistic on to your young folks.

Some parents would say I painted a rosy picture of real life in the above story of the young girl who ended up in retail clothing sales. They would tell you of sons and daughters who are thirty-five and forty who still have not found themselves, who work at odd jobs that are, in their parents' opinion, "beneath" them. These sons and daughters may have spent fifteen years resisting full-time jobs or settling down. They may smoke too much dope, be caught by cocaine, downed by alcohol, spoiled by association with bad companions, caught up in odd religions, be the world's oldest hippies, or glower their way through life as leathered punks with a touch of gray at the temples.

The moral? It could be worse.

A Look at the Prejudices of Parents

One thing I've learned from my offspring is that, as a midlife parent, I came complete with a full set of prejudices about what constitutes a proper job. Here, as nearly as I can see, are the full-on expectations that I have—or used to have before my offspring broadened my view of life. You, too, may think the same way about jobs. It's a mindset that doesn't comfortably accommodate what our kids may be doing. In other words, if you think old way (to be described), and they think new way (to be described), then a lot of judging, unhappiness, and family conflict can result. (Parents who grew up in the 1950s may be more likely to differ from their kids when it comes to cultural expectations than parents who came of age during the flower-power 1960s.)

Now, let's take a look at these issues, with the hope of avoiding trouble down the road.

The following is the old way of thinking, the supposedly "correct" pattern of a work life that we learned when we were young: A job, to be considered a "good" job, has to be a white-collar professional position, certainly full-time. It probably involves a briefcase along with steady paychecks and a full range of benefits, including health as well as retirement benefits that will insure a happy old age in Florida. (Dispensing with the briefcase is okay if one is a surgeon. It is always okay to be a surgeon, preferably brain or heart, though gallbladders will do in a pinch.)

Job-hopping, according to the old way of thinking, is the sign of an unstable personality. One should be loyal to the company, which will demonstrate its good faith and concern by providing fine working conditions, reliable employment, and steady raises. Good work will be recognized and rewarded by a boss who should be respected and called "Sir."

Such were the beliefs with which many in our generation were raised. Now, here, briefly, is the worldview of many younger people: There are many ways to work. White-collar jobs may be suitable for some people and not for others. Blue-collar jobs, in fact, can provide a good living wage, physical exercise, and allow the worker to leave professional concerns at work and enjoy the leisure of nonwork time. It is often healthier and less stressful, in fact, to have a job like a carpenter or landscape contractor than to have a desk-bound yuppie job that may consist of staring at a computer screen all day long.

It is, in fact, outdated and limiting to even think in terms of white and blue collar at all, given the complexities of today's work spectrum. After all, when Ph.D.'s drive taxis and your waitress at lunch today has an advanced degree in archeology, who's to say what's white or blue anymore?

Doing what you are happy at, whether white, blue, or no collar, is what life is all about. And why break one's back in a gray flannel suit for a corporation that will only be bought, merged, or go bankrupt? The end result of such corporate upheavals is often employee layoffs and cutbacks, a heck of a reward for the loyalty of years of hard work.

Don't necessarily trust the Fortune 500. Your reward for wearing their white collar may be a pink slip.

And that's a newer view of work for you to mull over.

You may also find it instructive to talk to young people about their jobs, because they translate this new philosophy into lives that are lived with gusto, if not conformity. Many people in their twenties and thirties have abandoned conventional work in favor of a life that's made to order for them and by them.

Take, for instance, the young woman who is now a waitress working the breakfast and lunch shifts at a seaside restaurant. She used to be an account executive at an advertising agency, working 7 A.M. to 7 P.M., too busy to take vacations. But one day she asked herself what a nice girl like her was doing in a life like that. She rethought her priorities and settled on a daily pattern that would allow her to have time for her husband and for the music group that she loved to play with. As a waitress, she finishes work by 3 P.M. She makes enough to pay her bills, sees her husband for a leisurely dinner, and gets a chance to make music at night. And she doesn't drag the day's work home and translate it into sleepless nights.

Or take the young lawyer who grew tired of the tyranny of sixty-hour work weeks and the race for partnership in the firm. Yes, she had invested much effort in law school and in the job itself, but it wasn't satisfying life work, at least not for her. Changing direction, the woman sought and obtained a job as a youth counselor. She's poorer now in material things, but her sources of real satisfaction are overflowing.

What the foregoing means for us as parents is that we should ease up on our old expectations about what constitutes a fine profession. If our offspring can support themselves, are staying healthy and happy, and what they're doing is legal, then they're better off than most of humanity.

One last caution: Do not push them into the profession of your choice. June Lim, a college career counselor, cautions parents against this common error: "Have them get to know themselves and their own strengths. Don't push them into what you wanted to do. It may not be appropriate for them."

The Expert Ear
and Career Exploration

What is the most useful organ when it comes to having kids? The uterus? The heart? The brain? All necessary, but what most parents seem to use the most, at least with adult kids, is the ear. The parents in the survey did a lot of listening as their young people struggled aloud with the basics of who they really were and what they wanted to be.

One parent said, "We listened every night to career ideas at the dinner table. It took over the conversation. I think we did right by shutting up and listening, without jumping in right away with our ideas or with criticism."

Another said, "One of our kids never talked much about what she wanted to be. She always knew. But the other didn't have a clue about careers. She was willing to take whatever came along until we started talking to her. We asked her what she really liked to do. That helped her begin to think hard about herself. She's gone back to school—a cooking school—because she likes to cook. She had never thought of making a career of it until we started talking. It simply never occurred to her that she could make a living doing what she loved. She thought it had to hurt—this making a living thing."

A search for self-knowledge as described above is certainly the place to start a job hunt, because those who approach employers with vague statements, such as "I'll take anything challenging," or "I don't care what I do as long as it's interesting," are dismissed as people who are too lazy or addle-brained to figure out the direction of their own lives.

Parents can be very helpful here, as a child buckles down to find an occupation appropriate to his interests, aptitudes, and strengths. Since the past is prelude to the future, parent-initiated conversations about yesterday's enthusiasms are useful when it comes to ferreting out possible professional directions. You can help by pointing out both positive and negative experiences from the past:

"Remember how much fun you had organizing the senior prom? And you were social chair of your sorority. Ever thought of being an events coordinator?" Or "You just loathed being class treasurer. Banking and numbers may not be your thing."

It's also useful if offspring will simply ask their family and friends what they think the young person might be good at. Often other people see our strengths far better than we do. For instance, people around me thought I would be good at writing before I had the courage to believe it myself.

Have you had the same experience? Personally, I feel that a sensitive friend with good "people radar" may be more reliable than an aptitude test.

If the above suggestions yield meager results, you can try another tack. Engage in friendly bull sessions with your offspring centered around such questions as, "What's always appealed to you when you thought about professions?" "Who have you met or heard about that you admire and would like to emulate? What did that person do?" When all else fails, you can even pop *the* eternal question: Ask them straight out what they'd like to be when they grow up. Sometimes the top-of-the-head answer here is the truest one, unedited by thoughts of what's possible, acceptable, or proper.

Also, when coaching your offspring, encourage them to reality-test their career ideas by interviewing role models—people who are already working in the field that interests them.

Mimi Bross, a career counselor at the Career Action Center in Palo Alto, California, says that parents should also emphasize that the first job will not be perfect. It is simply a place to start, not where your kids will spend the rest of their lives.

Another tip: Be alert for articles in magazines and news-papers that you can pass on to your young ones. Feature stories about people in this or that profession can light a spark in a reader.

In addition to home-grown counseling, your kids can find help in other places as they go about deciding just what identity they will seek in the work world. Many hit the library or bookstore. At the end of the chapter is an anno-tated list of books that may be helpful.

As for nonprint resources, some video stores are begin-ning to carry personal development/career videos. Your child may want to give them a call and check their stock. The same is true for libraries.

Go ahead and suggest the books listed at the end of the chapter, but in the meantime, don't let your kids forget their college career centers. Some of them can be very helpful. The good ones provide a wide range of services and a level of expertise that goes far beyond what you can offer at home. According to June Lim, assistant director of career planning and placement at San Jose State University, a good college career center will have a large variety of job listings, a compre-hensive career library that includes information about employ-ers, a range of workshops, and individual career counseling. Ms. Lim recommends that young people act assertively when using their college placement centers. After all, some schools have thousands of graduates a year and just one career center, so the timid could miss out on the services that are in great demand.

Some college career centers are open to the public for a modest fee, so if your kid's school has a mediocre counsel-ing center, he may still have access to a good one by paying a fee. (If you yourself are planning a job hunt or career switch, don't forget your own college's resources. Also, the open-to-the-public college career centers don't have age limits, so don't overlook them as a resource for your own occupational dilemmas.)

Another idea: Look around for some of the excellent nonprofit agencies that offer help with careers. Inquire to see if there's one in your area. They offer seminars, counseling, a library, and up-to-date job listings.

The methods above—family bull sessions, informational interviews with role models, reading, working with a career center—may or may not lead to a great ah-ha, a blinding and sudden recognition of one's true mission on earth, but they are useful in getting a little closer to the question of what kind of job to begin to look for. Just don't let this time of self-examination slide over into a do-nothing exercise in introspection; that is, I won't take action on this job hunt until I've figured out why I exist. This kind of thinking can put your kid into an existential stall. If you see him beginning to freeze into the permanent posture of a sitting Buddha, give the following advice: WE FIND OUR IDENTITIES NOT IN SELF-ABSORPTION BUT IN ACTION.

Now let's assume that the self-exploration efforts have paid off and that your kid has targeted some occupations. One next step, especially if your young person is still in college, might be checking out those ideas in the real world through an internship.

Internships

Internships are short-term jobs that offer young people a chance to see the inside workings of an industry or profession. They can be an excellent way to test a possible career interest before making a full commitment to a particular profession. Some internships are paid; some are not. Many are offered as summer jobs during the college years. Some are offered during the school year as a supplement to classroom work. Colleges may offer credit for work experience gained in certain approved internship programs.

One can find internships in just about every field—media, politics, health—you name it. Internships, however, can vary in their usefulness.

Some organizations make every effort to integrate the young person into the real workings of the group. Some don't. And some use the interns quite callously as unpaid slave labor that is generally ignored and certainly not instructed. These "interns" are used to help the organization's budget by replacing entry-level clerical people and gofers. This isn't a good deal: The trade is supposed to be your kid's labor in return for information or instruction.

One of my sons had a media internship that consisted solely of answering the phone and getting coffee for demanding TV personages. There was no chance to learn anything beyond who liked it with cream and who liked it black. He quit, with my absolute blessing. But then my daughter had a truly productive internship with a large corporation. They taught her a great deal: how they ran their department, how to use the department's computer system, how to teach certain subjects to employees, and, in general, how to behave and work well in a corporate environment. She is still in touch with the people in that company. Their recommendations have helped her get other jobs.

So tell your offspring to ask questions about what exactly he will be doing in the internship. And tell him not

to be satisfied with vague job descriptions such as "assistant."
He should ask how the day will be spent and try to judge if
the organization is just trying to get someone to catch up
on the filing or if it's making a sincere effort to instruct the
intern in something meaningful. If your offspring gets an
internship and is learning nothing, he might consider leaving, unless he needs certain school credits from the job. Life
is too short to be taken advantage of.

The college career centers should have information about
internships. Professors can be a good source of information, and
so are department bulletin boards and school job fairs.

Please note that internships (along with volunteer work
and part-time jobs) will help differentiate your kid's resume
from the thousands that pour into corporations each spring.
Internships can be a very effective foot in the door when it
comes to full-time "real" employment. So if your kids are
still in college, encourage them to explore internships.

Hints for You: Hints for Them

What should you expect during your kid's Great American
Job Hunt? And what can you do to help?

• Expect that the job hunt will take more time than
either you or your child dreamed of—six to eighteen weeks,
or longer, depending on the economy. And experts say it
takes a month of job hunting for every $10,000 worth of
annual salary sought. So you should not get discouraged if a
job does not turn up right away. (If you've been job hunting
yourself lately, you will understand all this in a visceral way.)

Also, if you agree to have your kid live with you until he becomes employed, don't be surprised if you remain a land-lady for several months.

• Expect that the phone will not be available every single time you want it. Junior will be on it making appointments for interviews, using his newly discovered deep business voice.

• Invest in an answering machine if you don't have one. That way your child will not miss phone calls from prospective employers. If your offspring has a funky message on the answering machine, make him change it for the dura-tion of the job hunt. Few employers will be impressed with acid rock background music or a flip message on the tape.

• Expect confusion, depression, and the blues from the younger generation. Low self-esteem comes with the territory of constant rejection. All those noes take their toll. Try and shore up his confidence. Tell your offspring that it's not unusual to feel like a down-and-out worm during a job hunt.

• You can help by making a space for the job-hunting efforts. Your offspring should have some place, preferably near a phone, to write and keep records of who was con-tacted, how, when, where, and with what results. These interactions are important to track. One of our sons kept a large manila envelope for each company he was wooing. The envelope contained information about the company and its employees, plus any correspondence and a summary of phone calls. It was a simple and efficient filing system. Access to your Typewriter or word processor is nice, too. A word proc-essor can change or update resumes in a flash.

• Tell him that applying directly to employers is the most effective way of getting a job. It is about twice as effective as some of the other methods such as mailing resumes; answering ads in newspapers and journals; using

71

private and public employment agencies; working with college placement offices; asking relatives, friends, and teachers. Experts, though, recommend working on all these fronts, not just one. (Within my own tribe, we too had the best luck applying directly to employers. College placement offices, private nonprofit employment agencies, personal contacts, and newspaper ads also yielded results.)

• You might mention to your young one that chance can play a key role in getting a job, so it doesn't hurt for your offspring to be out and about giving Lady Luck an opportunity to strike. Sitting at home waiting for the phone to ring does not put him in luck's way. I got my first writing job from an old friend I ran into in the common dressing room of a discount department store.

• Don't forget small companies with twenty employees or less. Most new jobs are with small companies.

• The average job hunter spends a mere five hours a week job hunting. That's one hour each work day—not much effort. Your offspring can do better than that.

• Tell your kids to let everybody know that they are looking. Someone might know someone who knows someone who is dying to hire the apple of your eye.

Resumes and Cover Letters

Okay, you didn't sign on as family secretary, but somehow your kids expect that you will know more about resumes and cover letters than they do. They may be dead wrong, but if you are called upon to give advice in the resume department, this section will give you a clue. (Don't forget, though, that more detailed help is available in the resources listed later.)

First of all, there is a spectrum of opinion about resumes. Some people think they are useless, or even worse, a sheet of facts that just gives an employer a good excuse to screen an applicant right out the door. For instance, a resume might show that the applicant spent six months at one job and six months at the next. Looking at the resume instead of the person, an employer, afraid of hiring a job-jumper, might reject the applicant instantly. No interview. No chance to explain that you had to move or that the company went out of business.

On the other hand, some young job applicants look at resumes as magic door openers. These kids imagine that if they write a great resume jobs will fall out of the trees. Who, they think, will fail to be impressed with the summer jobs they had, that they traveled in Europe, that they were captains of sports teams or presidents of school clubs?

Well, employers are not so easily seduced. When it comes down to it, what you've done, what you can do, and whether you'll fit in are the issues that will get the applicant a job, not a piece of paper called a resume. The resume is simply a starting point, nothing more. Resumes are not paper voodoo but rather work-horse documents that briefly summarize education, work experience, and interests, with work experience being the most important of the three.

Let's look at a sample resume in case you are drafted as a resume advisor. This resume is one my daughter and I put together for her after she had gotten a little work experience. She wrote the initial information on one page and I helped her put it into a brief format. The current preference is for one page only, though some people will spin out their life stories to two.

LUCY HESSEL

Street Address
City, State, Zip
Telephone Number

EDUCATION
SAN DIEGO STATE UNIVERSITY, B.A. in Athletic Training, 1985.

EXPERIENCE
ASSISTANT ATHLETIC DIRECTOR, Grand Champions Club, Aspen. Fitness testing and consulting; orientations for new members; individualized fitness training, including private aerobics lessons and weight workouts. Also organized tournaments and instructed group aerobics classes. Taught swimming, volleyball, trout fishing, and croquet. 1986.

SUMMER INTERN IN CORPORATE FITNESS, Shaklee/Fitness Systems, Inc., San Francisco. Conducted fitness testing for employees. Also taught daily exercise classes in aerobics, slow stretch, and circuit training. Conducted executive orientations in the fitness center. Trained to use a computer to track employee progress. Summer 1985.

CAMP COUNSELOR, Skylake Yosemite Camp, Wishon, CA. Taught water-skiing and backpacking. Cabin counselor. Summer 1984.

PROFESSIONAL WATER-SKIER, Marine World Africa USA, Redwood City, CA. Performed daily show, including ballet, stunt work, doubles, trios, and pyramids. Summer 1981.

SPECIAL CERTIFICATIONS
   CPR, Advanced Lifesaving, First Aid, International Dance, and Exercise Association.

ACTIVITIES AND INTERESTS
   Downhill skiing, water-skiing, horseback riding and jumping, swimming, fly-fishing, golf, backpacking, running, improving the quality of people's health.

Notice that the resume text is single-spaced with double spacing used to set one section off from another. Underlining heads or using capital letters for heads are both acceptable. Notice that jobs are listed in reverse chronological order, with the most recent placed first on the page. (There are lots of other ways to organize a resume, but this example is probably the most commonly used.)

Some resume writers who know exactly what position they want will include a professional objective at the top of the page—for example, PROFESSIONAL OBJECTIVE: Teacher of secondary school English or PROFESSIONAL OBJECTIVE: Dental hygienist.

References are not normally included on resumes, though you can put this following sentence at the bottom of the page: References available upon request.

If your kids panic and think they have no references, calm them down and have them think which professors or teachers might say something nice about them. Ditto for any summer employer or a supervisor in an internship or a volunteer job.

If the resume you and your kid have produced looks skinny and undernourished, you can flesh it out by saying more in the education section besides the bare bones data of school, year, and kind of degree. You can, for instance, talk about major and minor subjects and even detail some of the courses *if* they are pertinent to the job being applied for.

Have your offspring bring the typed resume to a printing shop and select a simple white or cream paper, called "stock" in the trade, on which the resume can be printed. (Using mom or dad's office stationery with the firm address crossed out will not do.) An order of fifty copies should suffice. The Yellow Pages list printing shops that specialize in resumes. You could consider giving the price of the printing job as a graduation present.

Also, have your offspring get some blank sheets in the same stock as the resume so he can type the cover letters on them and have everything match. If the printing shop has matching envelopes, some should be ordered. If none are available, the packet can be sent unfolded in a large manila envelope.

It's better not to send photocopied resumes. They look unprofessional. If you have access to a word processor connected to a laser printer, you can get excellent results. Some print shops offer word processing and laser printer rental on the premises so the customer can do it himself.

Your library certainly has books with more examples of resumes. *The Harvard Guide to Careers*, mentioned in the resource list at the end of the chapter, has an excellent section on resumes. There are ten examples. Each is the resume of a student just getting out of college, so they may be directly applicable to your offspring's situation.

Resumes are usually sent out with a short cover letter, not more than one page in length. Kids can get caught up in writing the perfect cover letter, so caught up that they draft and redraft it and thus avoid the harder work of job hunting.

The letter should be directed to a person by name and title, if possible, not "To whom it may concern." This is not always easy when answering an ad in the paper, but sometimes a quick phone call to the company will get a name, so an impersonal greeting doesn't have to be used.

Tell your child the text of a cover letter can be very simple, as simple as . . .

Street Address
Town, State, Zip

Date

Mr. Anthony Benisse
Athletic Director
Pine Cone Athletic Club
Address
City, State, Zip

Dear Mr. Benisse:

I've read about the opening you have for an assistant athletic director and I'd like to submit my resume for your consideration. I've recently moved to this area and have had one year's experience as an assistant athletic director at the Grand Champions Club in Aspen, Colorado.

May we meet soon to discuss your specific needs?

I'll call you in a week to find a time that's convenient for you.

Sincerely,
Lucy Hessel

And so your child should call in a week and try to get an interview.

If someone has been a go-between here, giving your kid tips about contacts, your offspring should mention the go-between's name (with his permission) in the cover letter.

Remind your protégé to write a thank-you note after an interview. A handwritten note is acceptable.

Interviews: You Can Help

No, we can't go with our offspring to hold their hands and answer the questions posed by the interviewer. But we can role-play with them at home, asking some of the usual questions so they can get practice at formulating intelligent answers. If you have a home-video setup, you can record the practice session and go over it together afterward. (There are sample questions you can use for this session later in the chapter.) When viewing the videotape, check such things as:

• Does the young person talk too much, monopolizing the conversation out of inexperience or nervousness? The conversation should be about half talking and half listening. If your son is doing most of the talking, or answering in monosyllables, something should change—namely, your son.

• Does the young person have good eye contact or does he spend a good deal of time checking out his shoelaces?

• Can the young person maintain composure and a pleasant attitude even when the interview questions cut close to the bone?

• Are there annoying verbal mannerisms? Check for "you knows" in every other sentence or the more juvenile "like" as in, "Well, it was like great." Double whammy: "Well, it was like great, you know?"

• Are there distracting physical mannerisms? These may include twisting the hair, scratching the scalp, picking at clothes, jittering around in a chair. Things like these can count against your kid, as can a sloppy appearance, too much perfume, sexy clothes, or the smell of cigarettes. (People are becoming so anticigarette that just the smell of tobacco on someone could turn off an employer.)

Now, here are some of the normally asked interview questions, and I pass them on in the interest of having you and your loved one prepared for anything:

1. *Tell me something about yourself.* Your kid should confine himself to the relevant here. The interviewer does not want to know his highest bowling score.

2. *How would you describe yourself?* Obviously, the

goal is to present a positive image without looking like an egomaniac.

3. *What about this job interests you?* Do not say the salary and benefits.

4. *What about this company interests you?* Better have done the homework. Get the annual report if there is one.

5. *What are your strengths and weaknesses?* Experts say tell your strengths outright—"I won't stop until the job is done," for instance. They also advise saying something innocuous and forgivable about the weakness, such as "I work too hard."

6. *What are your lifetime goals? What is your five-year goal?* This is a general invitation to make up fiction, but if people are going to ask such global questions, your offspring is going to have to muster a passable answer.

These are some examples of what people might ask, but what they are really asking is what your kid can do for them.

During the job hunt, these books may help:

The Harvard Guide to Careers, by Martha Leape and Susan Vacca. A basic reference book targeted right at the first-time, postcollege job seeker. It is well organized and has many examples of resumes and cover letters. The information is clear, useful, and comprehensive. It has good sections on career exploration and career decision making. Job hunting and graduate study are also covered. Since the above subjects are just touched on in this chapter, you can advise your young one to consult this book or others like it in order to obtain a more thorough understanding of the entire career process.

What Color Is Your Parachute?: A Practical Manual for Job Hunters & Career Changers, by Richard Bolles. Updated every year, this classic in the field is best suited for a print-oriented job seeker who is willing to put in time on the self-discovery exercises. Bolles's section on interviews is excellent and wise. If nothing else, this book lets the reader know that he has one understanding friend, Richard Bolles, whose humanity, frankness, and humor show on every page.

Wishcraft: How to Get What You Really Want, by Barbara Sher with Annie Gottlieb. This book is described on the cover as "a unique step-by-step plan to pinpoint your goals and make your dreams come true." It may sound like hype, but this book delivers. It is excellent, practical, wise, easy to read, fun to do, and very helpful in terms of clarifying what you want and exactly how you are going to get it. Think of this one for yourself as well, if you are contemplating a change or are restless with what you are currently doing. One of the book's strengths is that it takes what seem like impossible dreams and points the reader in a sensible way toward achieving them.

Your kid's job may not turn out exactly as envisioned. The career path may not be straight and smooth. Nevertheless, as the Rolling Stones say . . .

You can't always get what you want . . .
But you get what you need.

According to the 1980 census, two out of three young adults living with relatives are employed. Your chances are better than even of having that young person in the job world earning and learning.

4

Money and the Necessities of Living

What's the Goal Here?

As far as money goes, the goal of a parent is to produce sons and daughters who can stand on their own financially, take care of present obligations, save and invest for the future, and always have enough tucked away for taxes. That's the ideal, and, in fact, many of the parents I heard from actually said their kids were, on the whole, pretty sensible about money.

In these cases, just how did it happen that the ideal and the real weren't so far apart? Perhaps it was training, for there was one theme that ran through the financial section of the parent surveys: Make your kids responsible for money handling as early as you can. Some parents said they started when their kids were in nursery school, giving an allowance that was meant to be managed rather than squandered on candy bars. Most continued the allowance throughout the teen years. Many families provided children with a chance to earn extra money by doing special chores at home. During high school, it was common for kids to be asked to work during the summer. At college age, most parents provided tuition, room, board, books, and a small allowance. If kids wanted extras, such as ski trips or expensive stereo equipment, they often had to earn it.

Some parents reported widely varying financial behavior within the family. For instance, one offspring in the family would be a miser, another a spendthrift, and still another firmly in the middle of the spectrum. My own kids differ widely in this area. It is difficult to believe they were brought up in the same family, with the same environment and financial training.

Could it be heredity at work here and not environment? Just imagine the possibility—an aberrant credit card chromosome floating uncharted in the human genome. (Of course, it's not from your side.)

The families I heard from differed widely in what they would pay for and what they wouldn't, in what they considered sensible helping out and what they considered spoiling. Some are hard-liners, making the kids earn as much as they can and leaving it up to them to struggle with money. Others pay gladly for tuitions, both undergraduate and graduate, for vacations for the entire family, adult kids included, for car insurance, health insurance, and new cars as college graduation presents. Some even provided down payments on houses or condos. What interested me was that there seemed to be little difference in how the kids turned out. Most parents, whether hard-liners or helpers, described their kids as being sensible about money.

And that's the goal, isn't it?

Young Adults' Worst Money Problem and How It Leaves Them Vulnerable

For young adults, the worst money problem, quite simply, is that there isn't enough of it, not necessarily because they are spendthrifts but because they are using entry-level salaries to pay high-level expenses: rent, utilities, food, car payments, gas, car repairs and maintenance, car insurance (high in that age group), health insurance and/or health insurance deductibles, clothes, entertainment, furnishings, dry cleaning, and presents. If you consider what they bring home in salary and then look at what they must pay out, it's clear why they are not only often dead broke but sometimes in debt.

Their quiet desperation about money leads them to a pitfall that is rarely discussed: the vulture "employers" who will try in any of several sneaky ways to take financial advantage of young people.

These "employers" are greedy people who know that young folks are anxious for a first job and inexperienced in detecting scams. Some will try to hire your kids but pay them no salary at all. This is not the same as unpaid internships, which are usually clearly labeled as unpaid. There are employers who want to put out no money, take no risks, and let you support your kids who are trying valiantly to earn "commissions" to support themselves.

Typically, kids are lured to work with promises of extravagant commissions: "Why you only have to sell one of these gidgets a week and you will make $50,000 a year." Sometimes, to add insult to injury, they will be asked to work on commission but only if they will also buy the product for themselves. In our family, we encountered one company that was willing to hire our young one (commission only, zero salary), but only if she would first buy some expensive art (for an art gallery job). Then there was another company that would give our kid a job selling a health product that cost a thousand dollars, but only if she plunked down a thousand dollars first to buy the product for herself. One thousand dollars to get a sales job that had no salary.

And do not think because your kids are intelligent that they will catch on right away. If you bring them up to be trusting, they probably will be. It takes a while for honest and well-meaning people to figure out these charlatans.

Another way employers take advantage of the innocence of young people is to promise them a high salary and a lot of responsibility later on, if only they will take the low salary and the gofer position now. Somehow, later on never arrives. If the impatient young person pushes, she will be asked to move on.

And if you have a daughter, watch out out for the following: a newspaper ad that says "We Want Models" or a similiar come-on. When the young girl shows up for the interview, she is told that she will make a fine model and they just happen to have a photographer who will do her portfolio for only $700. He will probably offer to sleep with her, too. Free of charge.

Alert your kids to these and similar swindles. That's not to say all commission jobs are bad. Real estate agents work on commission. Many other salespeople do, too. But you should know that unless your kids are selling a good product, working for a reputable firm, and relying on you financially for a while, commission jobs may offer just one thing: experience in what not to fall for next time.

Now, let's turn from what other people might be doing to your children, to what you may or may not do for them.

Sorting Out the Reasonable from the Unreasonable

Just how do we parents know what is reasonable and not reasonable when it comes to money and the young adult? It was an easy call when they were in nursery school. We knew we were on the hook for everything. But now they're in that confusing stage where some help still may seem appropriate and some may not. The questions today are: when, why, how much, and how long?

There are no absolute rules here, for each family is different in terms of economic resources, the work situations of their offspring, and their values concerning money. We each need to make our own call on these issues. For instance, if you have deep pockets and a soft heart, you may well decide to help out with the first house. It would mean putting many thousands of dollars out the door as a down payment. Many families can't afford to part with such chunks of money. Some are strained just sending an extra $100 a month to their kids. Still others, while they could afford large contributions such as cars or down payments, wonder if they should give away what would otherwise be retirement income for mom and pop.

One father told me, "We've given and given. We sent them to private schools and good colleges and that's going to be it. They can worry about housing and grad school and school tuitions for their kids. My wife and I neglected our own retirement funds in order to give them a good start in school. We've got to take care of ourselves now. Look at it this way . . . by taking care of our retirement, we are making sure we won't be a burden on them when we are old."

This point of view is valid. Directing financial resources away from the kids and toward one's own retirement may turn out to be helping them after all.

Nobody can decide these things but you.

However, here are a few general tips that may help you navigate these waters. For instance, the following things could probably be considered reasonable (but only *if* you can afford them):

• Helping with graduate school tuition, if they are not eligible for grants or can't get financial aid of any kind. Just make sure before you invest that they are not going to graduate school because they don't know what else to do or because they feel safer as students than employees. They should have a clear goal and reason for going, for example, it is a requirement for their chosen profession (physician) or they will make a great deal more money over a lifetime if they do go. Also, if money is short all around, have them look into night-time or part-time programs that will let them work and go to school. Last, it may be wise for them to work first before going on to graduate study. It gives the possible MBA, for instance, a closer look at the work world before she commits to expensive graduate education. Furthermore, work experience can be a far more efficient teacher than books. Question any offspring who wants you to foot the bill for graduate education, unless both she and you can clearly see what good it is going to do.

• College graduation presents to help a young one get started in the business world. At the high end, this might be a car, either new or a family hand-me-down. Unless your youngster is looking for a job in a major urban center, wheels are an almost absolute necessity when looking for work or going to work. Yes, most cities have public transportation systems and yes, other people use bikes, but most of us, unfortunately, need cars. Other business-oriented graduation presents include a new business suit, a gift certificate for resumes and business cards, or a briefcase, but let them pick it out. They are fussy about avoiding "nerdy" briefcases. In the business world, you are what you carry.

• Helping them get their first credit cards or car loans. Some parents cosign for these. You have to know your kids here. They can, in their careless youth, flake out on you and begin to ruin your credit rating. This commitment is something to be carefully considered.

• Arranging private loans or gifts. This money could be used to buy a car, or to furnish their first apartment, or perhaps to purchase an appropriate work wardrobe. It could even be used to help them start their own businesses. Not one parent in my survey reported a defaulted loan, though a few said they had to remind their kids about payment. Some families had written agreements about big transactions, whereas the terms of the smaller loans were more likely to be verbally agreed upon.

• Paying for their car insurance and health insurance (if they are not covered at work). One family pays both these premiums for a son who is a freelance artist. He can't yet afford insurance and they want to protect themselves against what could happen to their resources if they had an uninsured son get ill or hurt in an accident. The mother told me, "We spent too much time and energy accumulating an estate to put it at risk. Besides, if the funds went to bail this son out of a major medical crisis, well . . . there goes the other kids' inheritance. It wouldn't be fair." It may make sense for you to protect yourself in this way, too.

• Helping with the rent to keep them out of low-rent/high-crime areas. One dad thinks it is an excellent investment in his daughter's safety to make sure her city apartment has a doorman, who, these days, often acts more as a security guard than a fielder of taxis. The father said, "Actually, I get more out of it than she does. She lives in a high-crime city and I sleep better at night knowing she's in a building with good security."

• Furniture for their first apartment. Many families use that wonderful on-site furniture store, the attic. Divorced parents who remarry often have duplicate household effects that they can give to the young ones.

• New tires. If they are driving around on some old threadbares to save money, you may want to loan or give money for new ones.

• Last, at birthday and Christmas time, the luxuries they can't afford for themselves: gift certificates for cosmetics and perfumes, nice clothes, vacations.

Now, if the above options are being suggested as reasonable, what's in the unreasonable category?

• Giving repeated monies to someone you suspect of drug use. If you have a kid with a runny nose, who's always wired and going broke, you may have a cocaine problem in the family. You do no good giving money because it will only go to the dealer. It's hard, but bow out and let your offspring go her own way, even if it means hitting bottom. Bottom is often the beginning of positive change. See chapter 5 for ways to handle substance abuse problems.

• Supporting someone who is making no effort on her own behalf to get a job, or supporting someone who is only making sporadic efforts to get a job. If you are already doing this—backing a born-again couch potato—you might ask yourself if someone who is half-hearted on her own behalf deserves your whole-hearted financial support. Expecting offspring to spend hours every day in job-hunting activities is not unreasonable. Stick chapter 3 of this book in her hand.

• Supporting someone who is supporting a mate or a significant other who shows no inclination to be involved in something as gross as the work force. You don't need to do a double dole.

Parents sometimes wonder when it is all right to rescue their kids financially and when they should begin to let them solve their own financial problems. Parents who are broke don't have to wrestle with this. There's nothing in the sugar jar. Correction: Some parents will go into debt to help an offspring. I doubt if I'd do it for an able-bodied offspring, but so much depends on what the kid needs. A bone marrow transplant, yes. A vacation in Paris, no.

The First Mistake Rule discussed in chapter 1 applies here. You should give your offspring the benefit of the doubt and lend them a hand the first time they make a mistake, but if they keep making it, sign off. They need to learn some lesson that your rescuing will prevent them from learning.

For instance, to apply the First Mistake Rule to finances, if kids get in over their heads because they didn't accurately gauge expenses versus income, it may be reasonable to make a loan if asked. But if the situation keeps happening, then negative experience is going to have to teach them what they need to know about money.

It may make sense, though, to help out in the following situations:

• They need medical attention, and have no money and no insurance. (Everything sensible should be done to avoid this preventable predicament.)
• They lose a job.
• They have some kind of life crisis: a divorce, or a major theft for which they had no insurance.
• They can't get a job. (Now this one you can argue about. Some parents think that if a kid can't get the exact job she wants, she should still work at something—anything—to bring in money. Wait tables at night, but contribute. Others say job hunting is effort enough and they don't mind supporting offspring as long as the job hunt goes on. The call here depends a lot on available family resources and values about the work ethic.)

For better or worse in this area, the choice is yours.

Getting the First Credit Cards

If you think that helping a young person get a credit card is like helping a baby pick up a loaded gun, you may be right. Nevertheless, credit cards offer certain advantages. You don't have to carry cash. You don't have to carry a checkbook and wait at the cash register for check approval. You usually get a float on your money; that is, you have the goods in hand, but haven't yet paid the bill. It is essentially a loan to you from the credit card company.

Last, a major credit card is increasingly a ticket of admission, for example, to instant cash, or membership in the video store, or getting your check accepted by stores that don't know you. In fact, the major credit card is now part of one's financial profile. What the driver's license is to your physical identity, the credit card has become to your financial identity.

There are disadvantages to credit cards, of course. They shield us from the reality of how much we've spent. For instance, if you spend $100 on a dress and charge it, it doesn't move you as much as forking out ten $10 bills—actual cash money. Green money acts as a spending brake; plastic cards have that tempting air of unreality about them.

But the biggest disadvantage of a credit card is the interest rate on the unpaid balance. Interest rates are high, more than 18 percent right now. It means your offspring will pay about a dollar for every eighty cents of goods financed on a credit card. Kids often miss this point, so you may want to mention it to them. Another disadvantage, of course, is that the deduction on consumer interest has been reduced to the point of disappearing, courtesy of tax "reform."

Last, many banks now charge annual fees, sometimes

as much as fifty or sixty dollars for the so-called prestigious cards. It seems silly to pay more money for a gold card, but financial institutions try to persuade us by offering extra services as incentives. Many of these services aren't directly useful or they have weasel-word fine print your kids should read. One expensive card offers to replace recently purchased goods (bought with their card) if said goods get damaged or broken. But the fine print says their offer is good *only if* the consumer's own insurance doesn't cover the loss.

Your offspring may not yet have been seized by these credit card realities. Do them a favor by passing on the information above before they get too intrigued by these little plastic rectangles.

Let's say, though, that they've considered the pros and cons and they want a credit card. How can they get it? If they have access to a credit union, they can start there. Or they can talk with a small local bank. If they get turned down, they can try a department store card or a gasoline credit card, both of which are easier to get than a Master-Card or Visa. You can also cosign for them, assuming that you have a good credit record. Eventually, of course, as they build a work history and a good credit rating, they can get a major credit card from a large bank.

And good luck to them.

"Stupid" Money:
An Answer for Being Human

When it comes to money, some of us want to go crazy, at least once in a while. Even the most miserly, even the most firmly budgeted of us, may sometimes get the urge to be silly. What silly means will depend on the person and some-times on gender. For instance, men might want to cut loose by spending money on a fabulous stereo, an accessory for the car, a fancy new saw, a wine cellar, or a sit-on power mower that makes them feel like the farmer their grandfather may have been. Women may be more inclined to blow money on clothes, jewelry, or new furniture. Of course, either sex may decide on the frivolities usually thought of in connection with the other, though I have yet to meet a woman who wanted a power mower.

Sometimes, these desires conflict and people in a family will argue about which nonnecessary thing to buy. One answer here is for each person—mother, father, kids—to have a "stupid money" budget. (This solution is only for families with some disposable income. If you have to spend all your income for necessities, the idea of stupid money must seem, well, stupid.)

I offer the stupid money idea to pass on to your kids—it may serve to prevent money arguments—and I offer it to you, who probably deserve it after all these years. Just remember not to spend all your stupid money on your kids.

Four Wheels for Junior

If there's anything that divides men from women, it's how they feel about cars. To me, they're a necessary evil. To the men I know, they are a power symbol.

The fact is, your kid probably needs a power symbol to get to work. Many of the people I heard from solved the transportation problem by passing down the family car. Mom and dad get a new model. The kids get the old. I have a venerable car, a VW Rabbit, that has been used for long periods by three young ones. When their cars break down, give out, or are damaged in accidents, Rabbit comes to the rescue. It's a good, natural solution—this hand-me-down car—as long as the car is reliable.

Sometimes kids have problems with what the parents want to hand down. Twenty-year-old males do not think that station wagons are cool. Some young women do not wish to drive a shift truck. If they don't like what you've got on the family used car lot, they have the burden of figuring something else out, not you.

But let's suppose they are buying a new car. How can they buy smart? And where can they go wrong? First, they should know right up front that intelligent car buying takes time. To begin, they have to define their needs. Do they need a super-fuel-efficient commuter car, a van, or a four-wheel-drive ski car? (Almost all kids will think they really need four-wheel drive, even if they live, work, and drive in a city. It's a more advanced version of the horse they always wanted, but you were too mean to get for them.) Defining needs realistically is the first step in buying a car.

Next stop is a visit to the place your kids used to call the "lyberry," so they can get to the magazines and books that rate cars, define models, give prices. *Consumer Reports* devotes its April issue each year to cars, so check it out.

If they're buying a used car or selling one, they should consult the bible called the *Blue Book*, which is usually behind the counter at the reference desk in the library. Put out by the National Automobile Dealers' Association, it gives wholesale and retail prices for different makes and models.

Your kids are wise buyers if they don't set their hearts on a single solitary make and model. They then have far more leeway in negotiation. Once they have selected a make and model, they can also look at *Edmund's New Car Prices* in the library to see what the going rate is for the make and model they want.

They should know that the sticker price on the new car sitting in the dealership bears but an approximate relationship to what they may end up paying. The sticker is more a wish than a promise on the part of a dealer.

Conventional wisdom says to shop in the late summer or early fall, when dealers want to get rid of old models to make room for the new. A car salesman also tipped me to shop on the last day of the month in the waning hours of the afternoon. Salesmen are then under pressure to make their monthly sales quotas and will more easily part with the car for less money. He also suggested offering 20 percent below sticker price and going from there.

Some salesmen try to muddy the decision waters by blurring three important but separate figures: the cost of the new car, the cost of the financing, and the price paid for the old car. This dealing makes it difficult to decipher what's really happening. Get these three separate pieces of information. It may take persistence, but only with these figures in hand can the shopper go to another dealer and compare apples to apples and oranges to oranges. Only then can she compare bank financing with dealer financing. Only then can it be known exactly how much the old car will bring in and if you'd do better to sell it yourself.

If dealers refuse to give your kids these three figures,

they should take a hike to the next dealer. Who has time for games?

Apartment Hunting, Apartment Living

First of all, know right away that how you would approach looking for an apartment may be very different from how your daughter may go about it. For instance, many of our generation think you decide where to live *after* you've found a job. You choose a home and a neighborhood in relation to where you work.

Well, it ain't necessarily so for this generation. Lifestyle issues can take precedence over work issues. Where and how they live may be more important to them than what they do. Example: They may not care what they do for a living as long as they can live in Aspen, or San Francisco, or at the beach.

Some parents think this approach is backward, but the difference in approach may reflect the differences in values. In the old days, there used to be such a thing as a "company man," someone whose life was dedicated to the corporation and the job. Well, the company man is disappearing as companies go out of business, lay off employees, merge, change, and offer early retirement so they can cut the payroll. The fast buck is king: Managers are rewarded for short-term profits, not long-term thinking that would encourage employee satisfaction and devotion.

The fact is, it's hard to be loyal to a job and a company when they aren't loyal back, when they literally sell out, leaving workers holding the bag and the pink slip. So the company man of our generation decided that one-way loyalty didn't make sense, and he evolved, in the next generation, into our offspring, who are cautious about committing to a corporation when the love affair is one-way. Instead of doing what the company wants, they may do what they want.

So, if your kids go about looking for an apartment with a mindset different from yours, though you may not agree, you'll know why. (Sometimes parents have to settle for understanding instead of agreement. It's not a bad middle ground. At least you can still talk to each other.)

Next, so you'll see why your kids may be frustrated out of their minds when looking for an apartment (and why they may ask to move home for a while), you should know this reality: Looking for living quarters today is like playing high-stakes musical chairs. There are always more people than chairs. Everybody competes for the same chairs. Someone always gets left out. And to add insult to injury, the chairs are expensive.

So how do people today hunt for housing? Through newspaper ads, sometimes through agencies that handle rentals, often by just driving around and looking for signs that say "For Rent." People who can take their time may pick out nice buildings and ask the managers to put them on a waiting list. (Some managers will even ask for a payoff to get an apartment in their building.)

Friends can be a good source of tips here, so tell your kids to let their buddies know they are looking. Super places, such as view apartments, little country cottages, pool houses, and carriage houses, seldom make it into the marketplace. News of their availability is kept within a network of friends.

As your kids look for a place, there's not a lot to coach

them on. Most of them will have the sense to get something they can afford in a neighborhood that's not full of gun-toting drug dealers. Different offspring have different fetishes. Mine like hardwood floors. Yours may like being near a running track or a pizza place. To each her own.

One common gripe after moving in seems to be noisy neighbors, so you might advise your offspring, if they like a place, to check it out in the early evening, when people are home from work and school. That's when the upstairs neighbor clomps, the kids cry, and the stereos vibrate at full and maddening capacity.

The other great desideratum is parking, but your kids have already figured that out if they drive and live in an urban area.

Your role when it comes to housing may be cosigning the lease, since the young person's credit is not always yet established. Just remember, if you are cosigning, that you will be responsible if your offspring loses a job and can't pay the rent or has to move across the country. Check out the provisions about subletting in the lease, so you have a way out of such a situation.

Another common situation occurs when you and your offspring are on the lease and there's a roommate in the picture, but not on the lease. Remember this: If the roommate leaves and stops paying rent, you and your offspring are still responsible for paying the landlord. Some landlords will not rent unless everybody concerned has her signature on the rental agreement.

Sometimes (as in often) kids will put down their parents on the application forms as references. Don't be surprised, then, if you get a query call from the landlord. If your kids are both polite and smart, they will give you some forewarning on this, so you can tell the landlord what a fine tenant he is getting.

Now, what, if anything, can you pass on to your kids about the lease itself? That they should read it carefully and add any special agreements made with the landlord. For instance, if the lease says no pets, but the landlord agrees to a cat, they should cross out the no pets clause and add the new agreement about the cat. Both tenant and landlord should initial changes in the contract.

Landlords often want first and last month's rent plus a security deposit. It is a sizable amount of money. If your offspring has no savings, she may ask for a loan just to get into an apartment. Sometimes parents give a gift here, especially well-off ones who are seeking to pass on their capital and avoid taxes. (Don't forget you can give $10,000 a year tax-free to each of your kids; $20,000 if both husband and wife give.) Some especially well-heeled parents will give a down payment on a house or condo, figuring their kids will be better off in the long run if they pay a mortgage rather than rent.

But before you make any major financial transaction with your kids, talk to your accountant to find out the tax-smart way of doing what you want to do. You may also want to call an attorney to ferret out any hitches before they occur. For instance, if you give a married daughter and her husband the down payment on a house, and she gets a divorce, what happens to that donated asset? Who did you really give it to? Does it belong to her or is it community property? Anticipating common problems can avoid trouble later.

∞

Now let's assume that Junior is in the apartment. The next step is to get some furniture in there, too. Of course, you can invite him to raid your attic. Or if you have moved to a smaller place, you can give him the pieces that will not fit into your new quarters.

If your kids need a desk, direct them to this great invention: Get a flat door from the hardware store and two two-door filing cabinets. Put the filing cabinets under each end of the door. Now you have a huge desk surface, plus four storage drawers. It's easy to color coordinate the whole assembly by painting it all black or all white or all anything. Or just stain or oil the door.

Bedding needs are more difficult to solve. Some kids just get a mattress and put it on the floor, dispensing with the frame and boxspring altogether. This plan gives them a firm sleep and an oriental look. Others are crazy for futons, the folding Japanese beds that function as both couch and bed.

Living room couches are expensive. In a pinch, your kids could use those extra twin beds you have. Piled in back with large pillows, they make an acceptable place to sit. Twin bed/couches solve the overnight guest problem too.

Coffee tables are fun to invent. Tell your kids to buy a half barrel, usually sold as a plant container. Then put some round glass over it. Import stores sell round glass in different sizes.

A heavy basket from the import store, also topped with glass, can be used as a coffee table too. I've also seen coffee tables made from shipping crates, hatch doors, doors from the hardware store, and antique doors. Or cut a small dining room table down to size, if it won't look too funny with short legs.

As for lighting, lamps from a business supply store are often less expensive and better looking than lamps sold in furniture stores. Somehow, lamps for the home have captured the imagination of the worst of our designers. And, of course, if your kids don't like what's on the market, they can make their own from all kinds of things. A wheel hub rescued from a dump can make a great lamp base. For hanging lights, have your kids again try the import store. Japanese paper globes are beautiful and inexpensive.

When it comes to kitchen stuff, your extras could probably furnish them with some basics. And what all of our offspring seem to want and use is a microwave oven. If their place doesn't come with one, you might consider it as a Christmas present. Microwave popcorn is so popular that kids consider it one of the basic food groups.

Before we leave the subject of the nest away from home, let's spend a minute on a roommate situation that may puzzle and disturb parents. Today, whether parents like it or not, girls room with boys and boys room with girls. I'm not talking about a romantic situation but a companionable sharing of the same quarters by people of the opposite sex.

We old fogies are not used to this. At least this one isn't. (My college would let men in the dorm rooms only on Sunday afternoons and then only with the door to the room open.) But times have changed. Now there are coed dorms and coed living situations. What really counts these days is not the sex of the roommate but his or her character. Besides, all kinds of surprising things can happen with these coed arrangements. My daughter is sharing a house—he on the top floor, she on the bottom—with a young man who is a fantastic cook. I go to visit her and get gazpacho or grilled scallops or duck marinated in honey, courtesy of the cook upstairs. So before you get upset about coed living arrangements, shake off that old training and look at the roommate as a person instead of a sex object.

Home Cooking Ain't What It Used to Be

No chapter on the necessities of life would be complete without taking a quick look at food. First of all, you may need to remind your kids gently that they have tremendous leeway in what they pay for food. You may expect them to know this because you did at their age, but you might have been a homemaker who read the shopping tips in *Family Circle* while the baby took a nap. Our kids are out programming computers and marketing car phones, not reading shopping tips the way we did, so they may need a little advice.

Their choices are these: They can eat out all the time and wreck their budgets, buy only at the gourmet grocery store on the corner and wreck their budgets, eat at your house and wreck your budget, or begin to pay real attention to the whole issue. Grocery bills can be cleverly pared down in several ways. First, by reading the newspaper ads about specials and then buying what's on sale. Next, by putting some thought into the amount of nutritional bang they are getting for their grocery buck. For instance, people who live on fresh produce and grains will have a much lower tab than people who go for meat and processed food. At the same time, they are eating more healthfully. It's one instance where price is not connected to quality.

When your kids go off on their own, don't be upset if they eat further down on the food chain than you. (Eating down on the food chain means consuming fewer expensive animal products such as meat and consuming more nonanimal products such as vegetables, fruits, and grains.) In fact, their less-expensive diet is far better than yours. Since it has few animal fats, it's lower in cholesterol. There's also a lot of fiber in a vegetable/fruit/grain diet.

Maybe you've already noticed that it's far more common now for young people to become vegetarians. Some parents react to this as if their offspring had run off and joined the Hare Krishnas. Not to worry. As long as they get some vitamin B_{12} and eat a varied diet, their food intake is probably healthy. Tofu (bean curd), along with an occasional egg and some dairy products, can take care of protein needs, which some nutritionists claim are greatly exaggerated anyhow. (These days some nutritionists are even saying that too much protein leaches calcium out of the bones.)

If your newly fledged vegetarian kids come home to visit, there's the question of what to feed them. Consider Italian food (pasta, salad, bread), Mexican food (beans and rice, cheese tostadas, bean burritos, salad, tortillas made without lard), Chinese food (rice, stir-fried vegetables, tofu), and my favorite, homemade onion soup topped with bread and melted cheese and served with a huge salad.

Of course, if you came of age in the 1960s as a flower child subsisting on brown rice, you will have little problem understanding your kids' vegetarian predilections.

When I asked parents in the survey if they had any good recipes to pass on to kids, those who replied emphasized pasta, pasta, and more pasta. And anything goes on top: stir-fried vegetables, sautéed seafood, pesto, canned spaghetti sauce. Also mentioned as mainstays were omelets, chile, and baked potatoes stuffed with anything—guacamole, cheese, salsa. Salads were big favorites . . . something kids don't have to cook. Also, young people seem to use tortillas a lot, either just warmed or rolled with canned beans as a burrito, or flat with melted cheese on top.

Although I usually counsel hands-off when it comes to the younger generation, especially when they're out of the house, I do have one son on his own who doesn't eat well. I admit I encourage him to eat better things, even specifying dishes that are nutritious and healthy.

Here's how you, too, can be a nutrition busybody:

MOTHER TO SON: Look, I know you hate to cook and you don't want to spend time at this meal thing, but there are fast and easy ways to get meals. For instance, find a supermarket or fast-food place that has a salad counter. You can be through that line in two minutes, having loaded up on three different kinds of greens, plus maybe a dozen raw vegetables, plus toppings. They do the work; you do the eating. Or grab a roast chicken at a deli counter; get some carrot salad and cole slaw at the same time. Pick up a loaf of French bread and you have a feast.

Don't have time to cook breakfast? Try instant oatmeal, fresh fruit, or yogurt.

Try eating out for lunch and make that your big meal of the day. Prices are cheaper at lunch and you keep your weight down better if you load up on food early in the day and eat lightly at night.

End of lecture.

This chapter has highlighted just some of the issues connected to living away from home. For a closer look at the nitty-gritty side of life—the one connected with the wallet—pick up a copy of *Betty Ashton's Guide to Living on Your Own* (Little, Brown). She covers in detail important issues such as taxes, shopping, utilities, financial planning, insurance, telephones, cars, and health care. It is also a good book for newly divorced women and widows who have not been used to handling these issues within the family and now need to guide their young adults.

If you try to pass on a few tips from this chapter and your children tell you that you worry too much about money, tell them what Joe Louis said: "I don't like money actually, but it quiets my nerves."

Here's to your quiet nerves.

5

Trouble Time

When Kids Won't Launch

Kids want to grow up—they really do. They practice adulthood all their young lives, dressing up like mommy or playing with little cars so they can drive like daddy. They build roads in the sandbox—civil engineers at the ripe old age of four. They play house, soldier, nurse, cowboy, cop, and movie star, trying on adult professions as easily as they try on your old hats in the attic.

The natural impulse is there. Kids do want to grow up. Why else would they measure their young lives in half-years?: "I'm five and a *half*," they say, relishing each chronological marker in the long march to adulthood.

But sometimes kids, especially kids on the verge of adulthood, march off the trail, follow the wrong path, and find themselves on a road marked TROUBLE. They may not know they are in trouble. And you may be oblivious of their floundering too, at least at first. But if trouble is there, it will usually be found out.

The problem could be chemical dependence such as alcohol or other drugs. Or it could be common illnesses like depression, or even the less common ones such as mania or schizophrenia.

About half the parents I heard from had kids with drug and alcohol problems. The children of another 15 percent had brain disorders such as depression or psychosis. These problems are significant. They are, in fact, major barriers to healthy maturation. After all, if kids are chemically dependent or have a brain disorder, they can't move toward independence.

Even if you have had no difficulty with chemical dependence or mental illness in your family, you may still want to read this chapter. Just in case.

Maybe you think you already know what to look for, but even very intelligent, well-informed parents do not know much about drugs or their physiological, medical, and behavioral effects. When I asked the survey parents if they knew the symptoms of drug or alcohol abuse, many left the space blank or answered in generalities. They said chemical abusers would be "disoriented," or have a "personality change."

Those things are sometimes true, but generalities are not as helpful as knowing specific symptoms. Only one parent knew the specific symptoms of mental illness, drug abuse, and alcohol dependence and she was a social worker trained to recognize these problems.

Dodie Alexander, executive director of a substance abuse prevention and rehab program for young people, told me that parents would rather hear that their kids were mentally ill than that they had drug or alcohol problems. Substance abuse truly frightens parents: Many of us will hide our heads in the sand rather than admit that Johnny does cocaine or that Debby is hitting the vodka every day before school.

The fact is, most of us don't know what we need to know. Besides being frightened, we are uninformed. We had little or no experience with drugs or mental disorders when we were growing up. The mentally ill were hidden and not talked about. Designer drugs were yet to be invented so none of us had then heard of the alphabet soup of LSD, PCP, and MMDA.

Well, better to be informed now than never, so let's take a quick overview of what to look for. The following information was compiled with the guidance of Reed Kaplan, M.D., former head of inpatient psychiatry at Stanford Medical Center and Robert Taylor, M.D., psychiatrist, author, and specialist in health issues as they relate to young adults.

Spotting Trouble: Symptoms of Chemical Use/Abuse

Let's start with what substances might be abused. Yes, alcohol and pot are the most common choices, but there are many other possible sources of abuse, from prescription drugs such as codeine to seemingly benign over-the-counter drugs such as antihistamines, which some people abuse for their sedative effect. Then there are street drugs: cocaine, crack, PCP, heroin, LSD, the menu goes on and on. People even ingest and abuse veterinary drugs, such as animal tranquilizers.

If this all sounds far out to you—something that happens somewhere else and then only to the ignorant, poor, and neglected—you may need a gentle nudge in the direction of reality. Young people from "good" families use/abuse a wide variety of chemicals: heroin, animal tranquilizers, cocaine in all its forms, antihistamines, mushrooms, LSD, hashish, marijuana, and, of course, alcohol, which is the most abused drug in America.

Just what are the symptoms of drug abuse? Of course, the specifics will depend on whether the person is taking an upper, a downer, or a hallucinogen, but, in general, signs of trouble are:

- Red or dull or watery eyes. Often a bottle of eyedrops will be a staple in the young person's purse or bedside drawer.
- Significant changes in the size of the pupil of the eye.
- Sleepiness, being "out of it," dreaminess.
- Being all wound up, hypermanic, buzzed. Kids may party until 3 or 4 A.M. or get no sleep at all for days at a time.
- Runny nose or constant sniffing.
- Weight loss (can be dramatic).
- Pigging out on junk food or not eating much at all.
- Delusions and hallucinations.
- Paranoia.

These physical symptoms will vary depending on the

drug of choice and whether the young person is intoxicated or withdrawing from use.

Next, look for circumstantial evidence such as:

• The smell of alcohol, many empty containers in the wastebasket, containers hidden in drawers, cupboards, the water tank of the toilet, and so on.

• The smell of pot in the hair, clothes, or room. Incense is often used to mask the pot smell.

• Smoking devices, pipes, metal cylinders called bongs. Even cardboard toilet paper rolls can be used to smoke dope. Metal boxes that strip bandages come in are used to protect the joints or cigarettes from being crushed. Zip-lock plastic bags are used to keep the pot fresh.

• Weighing scales: Your kid is dealing.

• Razor blades and mirrors. Coke is cut into fine powder with a razor blade on a flat surface like a mirror. Sometimes if no mirror is around, coke trippers will take down a picture from the wall and use the glass surface protecting the picture. Users can be so out of it that they will put the pictures back crooked. If your pictures are not straight, your kids may not be either.

• Drugs stolen from the medicine cabinet.

• Constant financial problems or missing money.

• Possessions that are missing: They were probably fenced for drug money.

• Phone calls from people you don't know.

• Quick visits to the house. These visitors are either buying drugs or delivering them.

Next, this circumstantial evidence is in turn often linked with changes in behavior both at work and home. Pay attention to these signs:

• Lowered motivation, poor work or school performance.

• Argumentativeness, difficulty in everyday human relations.

• Social withdrawal, wanting to be alone to take drugs, enjoy drugs, recover from the effects of drugs.

• Bouts with "flu" symptoms, which can really be a side effect of drug use.

• Lying, deceitfulness, forgetting, irresponsibility.

• Changed speech patterns. Alcohol slurs speech, pot may slow it, and coke can induce chatter or a perception that one is saying something profound when one is not.

• Silliness and much giggling. I don't know why the experts neglect to mention this, but people stoned on pot can either smile a lot or think everything is funny.

• Preoccupation with music, moving objects, lights. MTV provides the perfect focus of attention for the stoned spectator. The music, colors, and special effects are all heightened by dope.

• Accidents, with a car or around the house.

Just because a person is using drugs does not mean that he has a problem with major league addiction. But you will know that things have gotten totally out of hand if or when the chemical comes to dominate the person's whole life— work, school, family, friends, and outside activities. Addiction is present when a loved one has a constant overwhelming need to get stoned, high, or drunk. When your offspring will sacrifice health, wealth, and happiness to satisfy a craving for a chemical, he is in trouble.

One question zooms right at us here: Why do some people become addicted whereas others do not? Why can some get away with being only occasional users of drugs/

alcohol and why have others gone down the road to addiction? Nobody really knows, but it seems we are all metabolically different. Some of us can "take" certain chemicals and some of us can't. And not surprisingly, even our heredity probably plays a role in our susceptibility to drugs and perhaps our need for them. For instance, there's an inherited predisposition to alcoholism, which is why the children of alcoholics are at higher risk for the disorder.

What does drug or alcohol abuse mean to a parent trying to launch an abusing kid into the world?

It means that a child who is abusing chemicals is not likely to be doing well at a job because of a lack of motivation, social withdrawal, and frequent absences caused by hangovers or drug use. Since jobs are essential to independence, a kid may be stuck on your doorstep until he solves his problem of chemical abuse.

Another necessary element of independence is money. If your son has chosen an expensive drug to abuse, he may be handing all financial resources over to a drug dealer. So there goes the down payment on the condo he was going to buy.

For your offspring's health and your own survival an effort must be made to change the direction from chemically dependent into chemically clean. Where to begin? With that same old trusty device you've been using for years: *the talk*. But forget about trying to talk with kids when they're drunk or high. They are not themselves then and may not remember a word that was said. If they are abusing alcohol, they are also more likely to become argumentative. So try

to talk with them before they hit the bottle, smoke a joint, or sniff a line.

Do your level best to be calm and express your concern about their behavior. Be specific. Present what you see as evidence of trouble, for example, "You have come home drunk three times this week." Or, "You have all the symptoms of someone using cocaine and I found a razor blade on a mirror in the bathroom."

They may deny they are doing anything wrong. They may walk out or say they'll think about it. They may agree and yet not do anything, or agree and actually do something, like get treatment. So be prepared for a range of reactions.

If they are living at home, are addicted to drugs/alcohol, and are unwilling to change, use the leverage at your disposal. Consider kicking them out and withdrawing financial support unless they change and seek professional help. Giving them and their habit shelter is doing them no favor at all. Let them face the results of their actions without your shielding them. Often, encountering bad consequences in the outside world is the only way they will be jolted into action to help themselves.

On this one issue, it is kind to be cruel.

Treatment

Survey parents who had no experience with drug and alcohol problems were innocent optimists when it came to suggestions about helping a son or daughter with these problems. Overwhelmingly, they recommended love and communication. But that idealistic advice came from parents who hadn't faced the problem. They exhibited what I call the inoculation fallacy, a belief, indeed almost a passionate faith, that being a good and loving parent will prove an inoculation against catastrophe. Love your kids, treat them well, and you will reap the goodness that you've sown. At least that's how the script goes. But one thing is wrong with this thinking: It isn't true. Bad things not only happen to good people but bad things happen to good parents. And bad things happen to the children of good parents. Maybe even to a good parent like you.

Then, on the other hand, there were the realists of the survey, the parents who had lived through drug and alcohol problems. They were strongly in favor of structured treatment programs and self-help groups such as Alcoholics Anonymous, Narcotics Anonyous, or Alanon. They recommended *intervention*, not just understanding.

Where one will go for help or treatment is determined by several things: the nature of the addiction, the nature of the health insurance, the quality of the facilities, and whether in- or outpatient therapy is judged most appropriate, given the life circumstances of the person seeking treatment.

Inpatient treatment should be considered when

- The addiction is so profound that withdrawal has severe physical consequences.
- The addiction is complex. Several chemicals have been abused.
- There are severe physical problems caused by the addiction (liver damage, infections, and so forth).
- There are severe behavioral problems caused by the addiction (violence, hallucinations, delusions, suicidal feelings, suicide attempts).

- Outpatient treatment has failed.
- The family is not present to act as a support group for the young person. (The family may be so put off by the young person's behavior that they have withdrawn, given up.)

Most users, however, choose outpatient programs. These allow people to go through treatment without disrupting school or professional life and without the stigma of hospitalization. (Some people are sensitive about what friends and coworkers might think about a stay at the Betty Ford Center or Hazelden.) Outpatient programs can work well for intranasal cocaine abusers and for people who are in the earlier stages of drug abuse.

More details about specific drugs, detoxification, treatment, support groups, and aftercare can be found in *The Facts About Drugs and Alcohol* by Mark Gold, M.D., the physician who started the 800-COCAINE Helpline. (Call 800-COCAINE if you need help or information on this subject. You won't be alone. Within two years, the hotline had one and a half million calls.) Another resource is Cocaine Anonymous, P.O. Box 1367, Culver City, CA 90239. Their telephone is (213) 559-5833.

Obviously, treatment decisions need research, but sometimes the choice will be determined by the nature of your insurance coverage, not by you. To cut costs, insurance companies are discouraging the use of expensive inpatient programs and encouraging the use of outpatient programs. Some individual insurance contracts (as opposed to group health insurance obtained through an employer) do not offer inpatient coverage at all. And some insurance companies are getting tough about covering even outpatient visits. For instance, some only cover up to 50 percent of a visit to a limit of twenty-five dollars, which, given the high charges for visits, may mean that only 25 to 30 percent of the actual visit is covered.

If fate has handed you a kid with drug or alcohol problems please don't waste your valuable energy wondering where *you* went wrong. You aren't the one in trouble. You aren't the one stuffing cocaine up your nose. The generations who come after us will look at our culture and wonder where we got the peculiar notion that parents are responsible for everything bad that happens to their children. This unproved notion has produced guilty parents and kids who won't take responsibility for their own choices. It has produced mothers and fathers who, as Samuel Butler says, "seem compelled by unkind fate to parental servitude for life. There is no form of penal servitude much worse than this."

Of course, there are some extremely irresponsible families who collude with substance abuse. These parents may be significant abusers themselves and may pay more attention to drugs than to their kids. These dysfunctional families are in clear trouble.

However, you probably did not contribute to your son's alcohol problem unless you personally insisted on his drinking a quart of whiskey a day. You did not cause your daughter's coke problem unless you went out and scored a gram for her and served it to her in neat little lines. So don't book passage on the Great American Guilt Trip. You'll get shipwrecked. And if you need to smile just about now, try to imagine a culture the opposite of ours, a culture where offspring are blamed for everything bad that happens to their parents.

What a delicious reversal that would be.

Well, at least for a day or two.

Now let's turn to other problems that sometimes thwart the growing up process.

Recognizing Depression

We've all felt down now and then, but sometimes this depressed mood becomes persistent and overwhelming, what psychiatrists call a major depressive episode or unipolar depression. When a kid is depressed, he is very hard to launch. Everything seems very difficult to do: Energy levels are low. Ditto for morale levels.

Here are some of the signs and symptoms of a major depressive episode. Not all depressed people have all of them.

- Down in the dumps, sad, blue, irritable, hopeless
- Loss of interest in usual pleasures or activities
- Decrease in energy, increase in fatigue
- Sense of worthlessness or guilt
- Disturbance in appetite
- Change in weight
- Sleep disturbance
- Moving more slowly
- Diminished ability to think, concentrate, decide
- Thoughts of death or suicide, suicide attempts
- Reckless behavior, increased risk taking
- Drug abuse

Depressed people are not "crazy," that is, out of touch with reality. Their thoughts aren't usually way off-base: Their moods are. Depression may be caused by significant life events or by a wayward process of brain chemistry that seems independent of life events. Depressive episodes are common. More than 20 million people in the United States, roughly 10 percent of the population, will suffer a mood disorder during their lifetime. What makes this statistic doubly sad is that so many depressed people will not seek treatment.

What Helps

Depressed people are in fact ill. Their brain chemistry has gone awry for a while, probably a matter of misbehaving molecules. Yet many of these physically ill people will resist going to see a medical doctor—a psychiatrist—who can give them the very medications that will relieve their symptoms. (One route around this, incidentally, is to have your kid visit the family doctor or internist, who can prescribe antidepressive medications. That way, help is given, and the perceived stigma of going to a psychiatrist is avoided.) Another choice is to go to a biologically oriented psychiatrist (as distinguished from a Freudian analyst or psychotherapist). This type of specialist tends to be more up-to-date on the latest medications and the most effective doses.

As for what you can do for your depressed offspring, you should resist telling him to cheer up. It's well-meant advice, but depressed people can't change the biochemical aberration that's going on in their bodies. Telling them to cheer up is like telling a man with a broken leg not to limp.

The good news—you and I both need some here—is that depression is a very treatable disease. People can recover nicely and go on enjoy life again. And even while in treatment, many people seem to carry on their lives normally. Just they, their doctor, and their families know that they are on medication that is chasing the blues away.

Major Brain Disorders and What to Do About Them

We'll briefly review two more disorders—mania and schizophrenia—so that if you encounter them, you'll at least have a fighting chance of knowing what you may be dealing with. And it's not impossible that you'll run into them. Schizophrenia, for instance, hits one person in a hundred, so it's not a rare disease. And it hits just as the young person is leaving home. Age of onset is late teens for males and mid-twenties for females, so the disease interferes profoundly with the launching process.

In this brief overview, we'll look at symptoms, signs, and treatments and suggest books and groups that could be helpful.

Mania is characterized by an elevated mood that is cheerful, high, and expansive, though this mood may alternate with irritability or depression. Hyperactivity is a hallmark of mania, and much of this energy is focused on activities that are political, religious, social, or sexual. Increased sociability is common here, with manic people getting in touch with friends at all hours of the day and night. There's a grandiosity and lack of judgment associated with the disorder. People may go on spending sprees, drive recklessly, or become flamboyantly sexual or theatrical.

Besides this elevated mood, mania is commonly associated with

- Marked increase in activity
- Increased talkativeness
- Thoughts racing rapidly through the mind
- Inflated sense of self-worth
- Decreased need for sleep
- Distractibility
- Hostility
- Paranoia

Often the person with mania has no self-awareness of the problem and may, in fact, actually enjoy the disorder in its early stages.

Mania can be very well controlled with lithium and other medications. Lithium enables people with mania to live stabilized lives. The dosage, though, must be carefully monitored by a skilled physician to determine its effects.

If your offspring has symptoms of mania, drag him in for medical help, no ifs, ands, or buts. The disorder is treatable, but untreated, it can land people in a lot of trouble. They may spend their way through the local department store or be found directing Main Street traffic wearing nothing but their underwear. Get help.

Schizophrenia is another disorder of the brain. As stated before, it strikes young people who are just at the nest-leaving age: late teens to mid-twenties. It struck one of my sons in his freshman year of college.

The disease is very misunderstood. It is not a split personality, nor are people with schizophrenia more violent than the rest of us. That's what it isn't. What it is is a disorder characterized by

- Deterioration from a previous level of functioning.
- Disturbed and bizarre ideas. Delusions (being able to "broadcast" one's thoughts, thinking one is the savior, and so on).
- Disturbed logic. Speech can become disjointed and incomprehensible.
- Hallucinations, especially hearing voices.
- Lack of emotion or feeling. Inappropriate emotions.
- Disturbed sense of self. May feel controlled by outside forces.
- Lowered motivation. Goal-directed activity may be greatly diminished.
- Preoccupation and withdrawal.
- Reduction in physical movement. Weird postures. Grimacing.
- Reduced speech. Brief or one-word answers.
- Sometimes depressed, anxious, or angry.

That's quite a bill of no-good goods, and devastating for both the afflicted person and the family. However, schizophrenia can be controlled (but not cured) by medication, which is often resisted by the person who is ill. Antipsychotic medications such as Prolixin and Thorazine can keep the person out of the hospital and out of major trouble. For many people with schizophrenia, medications are the only way to reduce delusions, hallucinations, and bizarre behavior.

For more information, read *Schizophrenia, Straight Talk for Families and Friends,* the book I researched and wrote for families with schizophrenic offspring.

Anyone dealing with the so-called mental illnesses—which are really brain disorders—will also find help from the Alliance for the Mentally Ill, or AMI. AMI is a nationwide organization with more than 800 local chapters. It is a self-help group composed mostly of families who have a sick child. They offer information, support, lobbying efforts, and grass roots action to obtain better medical care, housing, and work situations for people with brain diseases. For more information, write the National Alliance for the Mentally Ill, 1901 N. Fort Myer Drive, Suite 500, Arlington, VA 22209.

Tips

Whether your youngster's problem is drugs, alcohol, or brain disorders, you as parents may run into certain pitfalls. Here are a few hints on avoiding trouble and handling common situations.

• Don't waste your time feeling guilty. Don't waste your time wondering what *you* did wrong. Your kids are not chemically dependent because you spanked them when they were two or because you had too much to drink on one New Year's Eve and they saw it. They do not have brain disorders because you toilet trained them too early or lied to them about Santa Claus's existence or grounded them for a month when they were teens.

• Watch out for professional incompetents. There are mediocre people in every field—in yours, mine, and the professions that deal with the problems of this chapter: medicine, psychology, and counseling. Try to get referrals from people you already know and trust, perhaps a family doctor. Or try the department of psychiatry at a medical school. When the problem is a brain disorder, people from the local chapters of the Alliance for the Mentally Ill can give you leads on good psychiatrists and treatment centers.

• Watch out for otherwise competent people who are just not trained in the area you need. Some psychiatrists do not know much about treating drug and alcohol abusers. Try to use someone who works steadily in the field in which you need help. And some psychiatrists do not enjoy working with people with schizophrenia or alcoholism—they prefer us garden-variety neurotics. So make sure your doc is comfortable with the kind of problem you need help with.

• Look out for professionals with antiparent biases. There are "therapists" who look upon the family as people who will sabotage the recovery of the client, your offspring. There are social workers still being trained today to think that parents cause schizophrenia. Though this is akin to teaching young geographers that the world is flat, it still happens. If you meet a counselor like this, switch to another.

• Be alert for counselors or psychiatrists who want to "cure" your child of mental illness by the *exclusive* use of talk therapy. While talking and sharing can be useful and comforting, medications are the key to treating the major mental illnesses. If you run into someone who wants to treat schizophrenia with just talk alone, run for the nearest exit.

• If you think that a change of scene will be the answer, you may be wrong. Although it is sensible to remove a druggie from drug-using friends and dealers, a geographical solution alone will not solve things. Going to live on the ranch with Uncle Bob, going to Europe with a tour group, or going away to school will not address the basic problem. One set of parents, in fact, told me about a religious boarding school run by monks—the kind of place to send your kid to keep him out of trouble, right? Well, in that school, many of the boarders come from South America and arrive with suitcases full of drugs that they proceed to sell to other students, thereby assuring themselves of abundant spending money while at school. So sending a kid away may mean sending him into even more problems. (Please note that I'm not talking about qualified treatment centers or aftercare facilities such as halfway houses. These places may be removed geographically from where you live, but they have structured treatment programs.)

These are a few things to watch out for as you navigate the treatment path. Now let's look at what role you might productively play when addressing these troubles with your kids.

Your Role:
It's Not Your Problem

Just what should be your role here? How involved should you get in helping a young person deal with drug addiction, alcoholism, and mental illness? Having asked that question myself, and talked to many parents who've tried to answer it for themselves, I offer the following guidelines:

Don't ignore the problem. Parents may be tempted, especially at first, to deny there is a problem at all. This is not surprising. These are scary areas—addiction and brain diseases. We may kid ourselves that the drinking is a stage or depression is just part of the growing-up process or that our kids wouldn't use drugs. The denial can be compounded by the kids themselves, who may also refuse to see what trouble they're in. So, first, try to identify and acknowledge what the problem is.

But you aren't the main figure in this drama. It is someone else's problem. You can tell your kid what you see happening. You can suggest resources for treatment and recovery. You can offer full support during this time, encouraging and understanding the effort to overcome severe problems.

But your offspring may refuse to go for treatment. Or they may go for treatment and relapse. Again and again. And that's your cue to become detached instead of ruining yourself with worry and trying to control the "bad" behavior of another person. It is not your life. It's someone else's and they are responsible for it, not you. If they need to drink a quart of whiskey a day, they will and you must let go. If they keep on wanting to commit suicide, the fact is they might, even though you commit them to a hospital to prevent it. If they really want to end their life, they can find a time and place. If they want to sell their bodies and their souls for cocaine, they will. And you can make yourself sick—literally sick over these severe problems—or you can decide to detach.

Remember, too, that the healthier you keep yourself, the more available you'll be to them, if and when they become willing to receive your help.

Melody Beattie's book, *Codependent No More,* has a wonderful section on what detachment is and isn't.

First, let's discuss what detachment isn't. Detachment is not a cold, hostile withdrawal; a resigned, despairing acceptance of anything life and people throw our way; a robotical walk through life oblivious to, and totally unaffected by people and problems; a Pollyanna-like ignorant bliss; a shirking of our *true* responsibilities to ourselves and others; a severing of our relationship. Nor is it a removal of our love and concern.

Beattie continues by defining detachment as releasing oneself from a person or a problem, ideally with love rather than with anger or hate: "We mentally, emotionally and sometimes physically disengage ourselves from unhealthy (and frequently painful) entanglements with another person's life and responsibilities, and from problems we cannot solve."

She goes on to give good news: "Sometimes detachment even motivates and frees people around us to begin to solve their problems. We stop worrying about them, and they pick up the slack and finally start worrying about themselves. What a grand plan! We each mind our own business."

Codependent No More is an excellent book for any of us who have gone off-track, letting another person's behavior affect us to the point of becoming obsessed with rescuing another or controlling his behavior. If you are always suffering your kids' consequences for them, solving their problems for them when they could do it themselves, meeting their needs without even being asked to do so, read this book.

So, then, what is your role when it comes to chemical dependency or brain disorders? Recognize the problem. Tell the person what you think the problem is. Offer resources and aid. Participate in the treatment program if appropriate, but don't let somebody else's behavior ruin your life. Easier said than done, I know, but slowly and surely you can cut most of yourself free from the unsolved troubles of people you love.

And that may be the best way to help them.

Now let's go to a more positive chapter, one that's easier on our nervous system than the subjects we've been dealing with here. For kids' addictions and illnesses can be hell on wheels for parents. As actor Martin Mull said, "Having children is like having a bowling alley installed in your brain."

6

Kidiquette: Manners for the Modern Parent

What Do You Say About Your Son's New Earring? (And Other Social Problems of Modern Life)

There are books of etiquette that tell you how to behave when invited to the White House, that detail the proper way to serve finger bowls or eat asparagus, that tell you how to behave on a business trip to Japan or what your personal stationery should look like, but the bookshelf is pretty bare when it comes to information about getting along with your kids. Where, oh, where is Emily Post when we need her to mediate the cultural differences in just one house—our house? What do we say when our son asks us how we like the new earring he is now wearing because Ed Bradley wears one, and right on television too?

Well, the fact is we're pretty much on our own when figuring out the social codes and protocols for dealing with those newly fledged young adults, our children. As one mother said when I asked her how she would handle a certain social situation, "I haven't a clue."

Many of us don't have a clue, especially parents who grew up in the 1950s. Parents who grew up in the 1960s may have an easier time today with their young folks: They were weaned on flower power, not Eisenhower, and so may be more relaxed with modern mores. Even they, however, may have trouble, for instance, if the daughter they named EarthSong back in 1969 today wants to change her name to Katherine so they won't laugh at her where she now works in mergers and acquisitions.

Whatever your age, however, you may have difficulty in situations like these.

• Your daughter brings home her new beau, a man whose work history and profession are shrouded in mystery. It is obvious to you that she is being taken in by a con man who is after just one thing—her hefty income as a certified public accountant. What, if anything, do you say to her?

• Your adult kids come over for dinner, but they behave as if they are five years old again. They push certain foods around on their plates, refusing to eat them. The difference now, though, is that they eat the vegetables and leave the meat. Heavenly rutabagas. They have become vegetarian while you weren't looking. (And this from little cannibals who turned up their noses at spinach, lettuce, and broccoli at the very same dinner table and not too long ago either.) What's a good solution to this clash of cuisines? And how do you handle their remarks about the poor cow whose murdered body you are putting in your mouth?

• It's November and family talk gets around to voting. It turns out your normally intelligent kid thinks your candidate is a turkey: Mother, how could you vote for him? and so forth. Do you take the bait and get into the Third World War? Or do you sit quietly on your principles, bursting several small arteries in the effort?

• Your daughter is leaving the nest to get married. She wants a Cinderella spectacular and she's using the old "I'll only get married once" routine to convince you to spend far more than you can comfortably afford. What are some sensible ground rules here? Are there ways to handle this without committing overdue infanticide?

• At the backyard cookout you're giving for old friends, your son's wife is breast-feeding and none too subtly. One of the guests, good old Charlie from next door, turns the shade of barbeque sauce when he discovers that mother's milk does not come from bottles. Should you let nature take its course or say something to rescue Charlie or what?

You can see there are things to handle in our brave new world that are not traditional problems of social conduct. They are, instead, mostly New Age sticky-wickets that would strain the diplomacy of even highly resourceful parents. This chapter offers some possible solutions—a few ideas on how to handle a world bereft of the predictable proprieties.

Changing Power:
Changing Protocol

Although it sounds Machiavellian, the course of etiquette is often determined by who has the power. For instance, the most important man at a dinner party sits on the hostess's right. For instance, the older, presumably more important person's name comes first when making introductions: Mrs. Oldfellow, I'd like you to meet Janet, my daughter.

Kids are pretty low on this social totem pole. In fact, they are relatively powerless when compared to adults. Everybody runs their lives and tells them what to do. They are not yet in charge of themselves, not yet fully empowered humans. But as they get older and more independent, sons and daughters begin to become ascendant and start to take control of their own lives.

Parents, if they are wise, recognize this shift in power away from the mother and father and toward the children. They treat their offspring accordingly, showing the same good manners and respectful conduct to their offspring that they would to any other adult person. It may seem a self-evident imperative to you—dealing with your kids politely—but there are parents who treat their young adults like stupid children. They put down their ideas. They don't listen. What young whippersnapper has anything of interest to tell them? These parents have not recognized that they are dealing with proximate equals. Their bad manners show it. And their kids' resentment of them reflects the whole unfair and demeaning interaction.

One counselor I talked with told me about a family she worked with where the father's idea of a relationship was calling his son names, to his face and behind his back. The kid was "stupid," "an idiot," a "nut case," and so forth. Not exactly the way to build self-esteem.

Sure, kids may sometimes do things we don't approve of, exhibit the judgment of four-year-olds, and not seem to deserve the respect accorded adults, but then sometimes we adults act a little childishly, at least now and then.

Are you saying you treat your kids well and none of this applies to you? Well, take a minute here to run through a quick good manners test.

• Do you listen, really listen to them, considering ideas that are difficult for you to swallow? For instance, will you listen to your daughter's feminist ideas, even though you may find them threatening? Or conversely, can you keep your cool if you were a charter member of NOW and she says feminism is outdated? Will you listen to your son tell you all about reggae music, even though you don't know why he'd like this "foreign" music when there's perfectly nice American music around like Rogers and Hammerstein?

• Do you have a double standard of manners? One set for them and one set for others? For instance, if you are going to be late to an appointment with your kids, do you call and tell them you'll be a little late? Do you treat them with velvet gloves the way you treat a business associate or friend? Or do you let them wait, thinking that kids don't care about time?

• Do you interrupt your offspring all the time, not hearing them out, either because you think you know what they will say, or disagree with what they say, or think nobody under forty has anything to say? Parents sometimes barge into family conversations like longshoremen. My guess is that we often don't have the foggiest notion we are butting in.

• Do you consult them on their preferences for pizza toppings or their views on the economy? They may surprise you by having both.

• Do you know what your kids do for a living? No, not just their job title but the actual content of their day: how they spend their time, who gets on their case, what the rewards at work are, where they hope to be in five years? Knowing these vital things about your kids may endear you to them because you have taken the time to learn about their daytime hours, which is more than most people in the world will do for them.

• Do you have a double standard when it comes to sons and daughters? Daughters can get mighty put out when parents treat them like intellectual lightweights while their brothers are treated like Einsteins. The boys are asked if they think the prime rate will go up: The girls are asked if they think hemlines will go down. Sexism is, among other things, not very polite.

We should ask ourselves, then, if our behavior has kept up with the reality of their becoming empowered adults, or if instead we've gotten stuck a decade or two behind the times. The question is, Are we up on our kidiquette?

When You Disapprove of (Fill in the Blank)

When our kids are born, something magical happens. We suddenly grow a complete child control system somewhere inside ourselves. This child control system has two components: approval and disapproval. The approval section of the system comes completely outfitted with an array of smiles, pats, and encouraging words. The disapproval section features frowns, shouts, spanks, and criticism. Some of us use the disapproval components more than the others, though why we choose the power of negative thinking so often is a mystery.

When our kids grow up, we are still using our twenty- or thirty-year-old control system. The mechanism resists being shut down. It's like a motor that sputters even after the ignition is shut off. It's like a weed that insists on growing through a crack in the paved road. So strong is this parental force, this desire to give opinions, directions, frowns, and cautions, that if we harnessed its power, it could run the day-care centers of the world through the next century.

One mother told me she didn't know how powerfully her family's approval/disapproval training affected her kids until she noticed that her young-adult daughter would call home to check out every decision: where to live, what car to buy, and so forth. This woman decided she and her husband had overemphasized the importance of parental approval. They are now working on having the young woman make up her own mind. They're also teaching themselves not to intervene and judge everything their daughter does.

When it comes to parental power, a funny irony exists: The more we use raw-knuckle power, the more we lose it. Use it *and* lose it. Parents who push and shove their adult kids will find their power over their children diminishing, for healthy humans tend to ignore and avoid those who try to control them. Push and shove your adult kids and you'll find yourself shoved right out of their lives.

But potent is the parent who, though deeply interested in the lives of his offspring, keeps pretty much hands off. These parents have the most irresistible power in the world—power that is given to them by their kids, accorded willingly and with love. If we want to be respected, we've got to earn it by our behavior: It's the same message we've been giving our kids for more than twenty years.

Does it mean we must never say anything negative to our kids? That we must *always* be quiet, even if they are about to hang themselves one way or another? May I suggest the Over-the-Cliff Rule, mentioned in an earlier chapter, as a guide on this subject for both parents and kids. The rule is this: Generally shut up about the other person's life until and unless you see him about to fall over a precipice.

Then it's time to speak up. One example: If you don't like the fact that your daughter has no schedule when feeding her new baby, be quiet. It's none of your business unless asked. But, if you have a daughter with her first toddler and that daughter has not yet learned to turn the handles of cooking pots inward away from the edge of the stove, then you should speak up. You may save a curious baby a painful burn.

Of course, the Over-the-Cliff Rule goes both ways. Your

daughter may not like the kind of bedtime stories you tell her little Tiffany. The young mom may feel the Cinderella story fosters unreal expectations about love. But she is a wise daughter if she lets it go. However, if she sees that you are leaving bleach and poisons out where her toddler can get at them easily during a visit to grandma's house, then your daughter should speak up.

There is, however, a way to make suggestions without coming on as gangbusters, and that is to present alternatives for the consideration of your offspring: offering ideas about different ways of solving a problem. By offering alternatives instead of a single parent-sponsored solution, you're not backing the kids into a corner where they think they have to do it your way. And kids sure don't like it when parents say, My way or the highway—meaning do what I say or take a hike. Alternatives give them a buffet of choices. Anyhow, what parents can be sure enough of their own infallibility that they can offer a single solution as being the one absolute truth?

The bottom line here is that we have a hard enough time running our own lives without running someone else's.

In summary, when you don't approve, commonsense etiquette suggests that you keep your opinion to yourself unless asked or unless it's an over-the-cliff situation. Tell the kids you expect to be treated similarly. No criticisms of the dress you bought, the way you wear your hair, the company you work for, your diet, religion, politics, or passions—unless comment is invited.

And be quiet about about your son's earring: Your silence will drive him crazy. (And no, you can't tell him he looks like Elizabeth Taylor in drag.).

Food Fights

Gee, it must be nice to live in a simple agricultural society where everybody eats the same things. Yams and rice again tonight, kids. Or pease porridge hot. Or corn tortillas and beans. But, no, we are drowning in choices: Tex-Mex, Cajun, Vegan, Californian, French, Indonesian, Japanese, Italian, Mexican, and so forth and so forth.

When it comes to choosing among these foods, what strains family relations is that one way of differentiating yourself from your parents is in the choice of foods. I don't eat what my parents eat. My kids don't eat what I eat. We have three-generational cuisine: meat loaf for grandpa, sole for Pop, and sushi for Junior. So how do you behave when you eat out together or eat at one another's house? Can steak and potatoes coexist with raw fish?

If dining out, go to a restaurant that has something for everyone and thank your stars for pasta, the great conciliator. And if dining at their house, do not ask if the raw fish in their sushi came from the bait store. Do not say, "We used to troll with that stuff, not eat it." Do not speak about the parasites that lurk in uncooked fish. Do not say grandma would roll over in her grave to see her descendants stray so far from the verities of meatloaf.

And when the kids are dining chez vous and they say the beef at your table was cruelly murdered—they won't eat it—the most you should do is make mischief by asking them if their shoes and belt are made of leather. If so, of course it means they themselves are accessories to cow slaughter, to premeditated bovicide. And if their shoes are made of plastics, they are depleting the planet's oil reserves and contributing to the chance of an oil war in the Middle East. So there. (Sometimes we have to fight back.).

Another source of friction between generations when it comes to food is mother's feeling that her new daughter-in-law (or her son's cohabiteur) is not feeding him right. In fact, she may not be feeding him at all. They may eat every meal out.

Now we who were trained to feed our men think this is a kind of moral lapse. Why doesn't she make him a home-cooked meal? Doesn't she know the first commandment?: dinner on the table at six? Is she trying to starve him? All she makes for dinner is reservations. And so on.

Well, it's a takeout culture now. Women who work all day don't want to cook all night. Most of us did not have full-time jobs in the fifties and sixties. If we had anything, it was often regarded as a jobette, a cute little way to spend time that provided us with a few extras. Today, the work of these young women is paying the mortgage or keeping the couple from being evicted. So go easy on the daughter-in-law. And your son has not yet been diagnosed with malnutrition, has he?

Value Clashes

You may already be familiar with value clashes between the generations, especially those over money. For instance, if your parents scrimped through the Depression, then they most likely made do with what they had. They may never have thrown anything out. They may have saved string, old clothes, outdated furniture, and old kitchen appliances because "you never can tell." And they may have gotten on your case if you didn't make do, if you threw things out or gave them away. Not surprisingly, money has remained one of the main arenas where the wars over values are fought. For instance, we clash with our kids about how they spend their money. We can't believe they spend fortunes on cars, electronic doodads, elaborate weddings, restaurant meals, and vacations when they could be saving for the down payment on a house.

On a humbler level, many women from my generation—we who used to read and clip the weekly grocery store specials from the newspaper—cannot believe that our daughters do not want to drive all over town to pursue the best deal on bulk toilet paper. Instead of criticizing here, maybe we should rejoice that the lives of women have improved so much that today's young women have interests beyond good deals on toilet paper.

Money and its spending is not the only arena where our values may clash with our children's. No, we have many rich fields to fight over: politics, haircuts, religion, sex, TV programs, work, music, life planning, living together, sex roles (what a man should do, what a woman should do), and many other issues. Just about anything can become a bone of contention if we let it.

Well, consider these differences not as an inevitable threat but as a door to discussion and understanding. You probably won't change their values, but it would be interesting to hear why they have them and to explain yours to them, to tell just why you think house down payments are more important than present pleasures. And it is also fascinating to ask ourselves just why some of our kids have trouble deferring gratification. Why do they have difficulty saying no to the economic temptations of today?

It may have something to do with how we brought them up. Child-rearing practices of the fifties and sixties were geared to not frustrating the child. If we frustrated children and made them unhappy, we would warp them, at least that's how the theory went. Many of us believed the "experts" and went on to rear kids who were not denied anything of significance.

Like it or not, we were sold a bill of goods we didn't bother to examine very carefully. So now, we shouldn't be surprised that we reap what we sow. Yes, we didn't know where those child-rearing practices were leading, and yes, we were doing the best we knew how, but many of our kids were clearly *underdeprived*. And they see no reason now to start off on a life of hardship.

This realization, this seeing the connection between how they were reared and what they do now, doesn't solve the value clash, but it does make it easier to understand. And it helps to know that our kids are in there with us too, trying to make the best of their upbringing. For being given so much has been a clear disadvantage to our youngsters. Some young people are insightful and see this. One young woman told me that how she was raised—let's give little Dorothy anything she wants—is a real drawback. She can't, on her own, afford anything close to what her parents gave her. That's a real disincentive to independence.

As far as handling the value clashes between generations, I'd like to offer a solution that has helped me. It's an effective principle I discovered when trying to figure out another problem: how to get along with the opposite sex.

Let me begin at the beginning here and lead you along a road that was useful to me. . . .

The key to getting along with the opposite sex is to rid yourself of the notion that they are like you. They are not like you. The opposite sex grew up in essentially a different culture, with different expectations, heroes, interests, and goals. Linguists even say we speak differently. Women tend to ask questions. Men make statements. Two sexes, two cultures.

Once you accept the opposite sex as a different culture, you are almost home-free in terms of understanding and accepting them. Why? Because we instinctively don't waste time wishing a Frenchman were like a Brazilian. We expect them to be different. We allow for the differences in our thinking and judgments, just because we know they are from another culture. And once we rid ourselves of unrealistic expectations, we free ourselves from disappointment and resentment.

And so it is with our kids: They are culturally different from ourselves. They grew up in another time. The 1960s, 1970s, and 1980s, their cradle of culture, were not like the 1930s, 1940s, and 1950s, our cradle of culture. We might as well be from different lands as far as our values and expectations go.

It's funny. Parents can understand that teenagers are from a different culture, but somehow may have trouble handling the fact that their grown-up offspring are not chips off the old block. But if we recognize, even expect those differences right up front, we will not be disappointed when our adult offspring are not just like us.

The Killers:
Insecurity and Competition

Within the family lurk at least two nasty things that can contaminate good relationships between the generations. They are insecurity and competition. On whose part? On our part.

The scenario begins with an insecure parent, someone who, for one reason or another, doesn't feel very good about herself. One way out from these inferior feelings is to pick someone to feel superior to. Often people use other races: "Those damn XXXXXs are so stupid (or lazy, crazy, wicked, aggressive)."

Sometimes insecure people pick the opposite sex to feel superior to: "Men are such babies," or "Women are such bubblebrains." And sometimes, alas, people pick their children to feel superior to. This last is certainly an easy choice because even the most incompetent adult can convince himself he is superior to a little kid.

Insecure mothers and fathers use a variety of behaviors to reinforce their own frail egos. For instance, some use steady criticism. They tell their kids they are dumb, bad, stupid, idiotic. Of course, this makes the parent feel smart, good, bright, and knowing. These parents put down their kids' ideas and achievements, often comparing their own presumably superior record to their kids' inferior one. This is the parent who uses a lot of sentences that begin with "When I was your age . . ."

Constant negative criticism is more than impolite. It's a real crippler of developing young people and a block to the self-esteem necessary for starting out on their own.

143

Critical behavior is easy to spot: Almost all of us can tell when someone is chewing out another. We shrink inside when we hear it. But what's harder to spot is another behavior that parents use to shore up their egos: competing with their own children, surely a hollow victory for the bigger, older folks.

Parents compete in several arenas:

• *Athletic.* Dad always has to show Sonny that Sonny's backhand can't compare to his.

• *Looks.* Mama is in white-heat competition here. She is still wearing short skirts at fifty, flirting with her daughter's boyfriends, and running to the plastic surgeon every five years to get the wrinkles out. She criticizes her daughter's figure, clothes, and makeup.

• *The Domestic Front.* Mom is the champ cook of the house. When offspring try to experiment with cooking, they are herded out of the kitchen. Mother doesn't like anybody else in there. And mother is so insecure that she will not give her recipes to anybody. Sharing means giving the competition one leg up.

• *The Work Front.* Dad keeps telling his kids how they have no business sense. (They probably don't. They're young.) But dad won't pass on his business wisdom. He uses it instead to look good compared to his inexperienced offspring.

Competition in order to inflate a frail parental ego is destructive. The kids lose, because they are put down and not encouraged or coached to be their best. They also come to regard their parents as unpleasant rivals, not friends. The parents lose because they are in a no-win situation. Whether they want to or not, they will grow old and unathletic and

144

wrinkled and too tired to wage wars about supremacy in the kitchen or on the tennis court. Time will see that they lose the races they've set for themselves.

The parents also lose because what they are doing is negative, even evil, for it is evil to warp the positive growth of a young person. It must also be hell on parental self-esteem to know the only way they can feel superior is by competing with the young and inexperienced.

Though inappropriate competition is a breach of healthy human relations between parent and child, this issue goes beyond etiquette. Parents who make the home an arena where they must win are risking more than the accusation of being a bust at basic good manners. They risk losing the kind regard of their children.

The Peacemaker: Communication

If competition is bad, communication is its opposite—good. Much has been said in this book about the importance of a well-exercised parental ear. Hoping to practice what I preached as I was writing this book, I had several group bull sessions with young people, asking them to tell me what they wanted their parents to know about sustaining good relationships between the two generations. Let me summarize their concerns: Chances are that what's on their minds might be on the minds of your offspring, too.

• Don't do everything for us. We want to make our own decisions.

• Give us moral support even when you don't agree with us.

145

- Don't give us long lectures about why you're right.
- Be informed about drugs.
- Stop using guilt to manipulate us: "You let me down. You should be ashamed. That was the stupidest thing you ever did."
- When it comes to choosing a profession, allow us to follow our hearts.
- If you don't get high-handed and *insist* we visit you, we probably will.
- When you won't let my significant other sleep over at your house, we both feel you're rejecting us.
- Communication is two ways. Don't expect us to do all the calling and keeping in touch. Why don't you pick up the phone and give us a call now and then?
- Pay more attention to the environment. Help us deal with the problem. We're the ones who are inheriting the global mess and it's very much on our minds.

We've already addressed most of their points in this book, with the exception of their concern about the environment.

One way to respond to this issue and to do some good in the world at the same time is to give them memberships in organizations concerned with environment and overpopulation. For instance, memberships make significant birthday presents. My kids have liked these gift enrollments. And we can also take action by recycling or volunteering for environmental groups.

You and Their Romantic Relationships

When it comes to children's love interests, the social role of parents is hands-off and polite, unless the young one is dating a drug dealer, in which case parents may be as disagreeable as they can manage. Parents should listen and not interfere with romance unless it's to voice an honest if diplomatic opinion when asked. Mostly, however, you can count on their not asking because they sense you'd tell 'em. Anyhow, we let our kids know in other ways when we don't like the new steady.

Parents say, "Why don't you date a few other people too?" And they say, "Jim's all right, dear, but you can do better."

On the other hand, when parents think it's time their kids settle down with X, Y, or Z, they say, "Look at this wedding dress. Isn't it beautiful?" Or "Gilda's daughter is getting married next month. Wasn't she behind you in school?"

So our kids don't have to ask us. We tell them whether we know it or not. But sometimes they will ask and it sure puts us in a bind. If you tell your son Jack that you hate his girlfriend Jill, and he marries her anyway, he and you will always know what you think of Jill. So may Jill if Jack decides to tell her. On the other hand, if you say nothing negative—wild horses couldn't drag it out of you—and the marriage fails, you may be haunted by the feeling you should have spoken up.

Just know that you walk on eggs here. When in doubt, shutting up is probably a wise policy. After all, you wouldn't like it if they told you what was wrong with your mate and how you could have done better.

No section on romantic relationships would be complete without a discussion of sexual sleep-overs: having your child bring home their significant other for an overnight stay. We said earlier in the book that it's a private call, but let me pass on to you some of the feelings expressed by the young people I talked with on this subject.

Some of them thought that since the home was the parents' home, the parents should have the say-so about sleeping arrangements. If mom and dad are more comfortable putting the young couple into two rooms, these kids could go along with it. After all, it's only for a night (and some of them sneak through the dark to bundle up together anyhow).

Others, especially female others, were bitter about their parents' refusing to offer them double sleeping accommodations. "They make me feel like a slut," said one young lady. "When I bring the man I love home and they don't want us to sleep together, I feel as though they don't accept us."

When we discussed solutions to this sleep-over problem, all agreed that when parents knew, liked, and trusted the opposite sex guest in question, the problem seemed to disappear. The person became a nice human in parental eyes and not a threatening seducer, so everyone began to relax. The double bed then got perceived as a natural convenience rather than a moral lapse. On the other hand, when parents did not like the boyfriend or girlfriend, they certainly did not like double sleeping arrangments under their roof.

Another solution used by the young folks is to stay at a nearby hotel while visiting parents. They bypass the issue entirely.

Let's proceed to the etiquette connected with the next logical step in the launching of kids: marriage.

Avoiding Bloodshed at Weddings

Weddings have been a time-honored way to empty the nest, but the truth is that today the young couple often has set up a nest before getting married. Nevertheless, tradition lingers and parents still regard a wedding as the ultimate launching into the world.

How parents get through this launching is the next question. One way is to have no opinion. No opinion about wedding dates, churches, receptions, dress colors, flowers, food, photographers, or honeymoons. The happy couple is already surrounded by friends and family who are flinging opinions their way like handfuls of rice. Be thou distinguished by keeping your counsel. For the world will not be a far, far better place if you start campaigning for ice-blue bridesmaids' dresses or birds of paradise for the bridal bouquet, if that isn't what the bride has in mind. If you find yourself getting miffed over the colors of the table linen or the kind of champagne glasses the caterer uses, then ask yourself if these concerns are really the best use of your time on earth.

But if the bride wishes to bankrupt you, it is your right to say no. Remember, responsibility and authority should be equal. If she wants a $25,000 wedding, she can earn it herself. Of course, she will be older then, but silver hairs can look lovely on the mature bride.

149

Afterword

I write the books I want to read.

I write because I want to learn something. Books are great teachers, not only for the reader but for the writer. What I have learned with this book deserves a summary here, so the final meanings of these chapters will be clear to both of us.

I'll begin with what I have unlearned first, because sweeping away leftover myths and shreds of outdated beliefs freshens the mind and fulfills our kids' wish that we get "up-to-date."

About ten years ago, like many parents then, I wondered if it were "normal" to have the kids back home for a while after college. Was I stunting their precious growth? Were they stunting mine? Was I jumping right back into some now inappropriate mommy bag? Was this living at home really okay?

After all, American-style growing up, at least in our

generation, meant leaving the family, getting out, good-bye momma, good-bye papa, and so long to home sweet home. But there were my kids, coming back. And there we were, all enjoying it. Gosh, what was wrong with us? We were having a good time. Everybody was helping everybody else. It felt perfectly fine.

It was perfectly fine. Everything turned out okay, probably because, without knowing it, we were following the principles outlined in this book. All my kids are now on their own, independent young people but with ties of family affection that I would envy if I were on the outside looking in. Since I am on the inside looking out, I'm Grateful with a capital G. Furthermore, it's my feeling that our family ties were strengthened by knowing each other as adults, by having a chance to appreciate each other day to day, grown-up to grown-up.

So I learned that the received American wisdom just ain't necessarily so. It is not necessarily bad or a burden for kids to come home for a while. For us, and for some of the families in this book, living with a young adult is not only fine but if done intelligently it can be rewarding all around.

While writing this book I also learned to question the whole notion of independence. Independence may not be so much a matter of geography, of where one lives or with whom. It may be more a matter of internal physics: the private forces that impel one to action. For instance, if one listens to some deep interior voice and lives life accordingly, then one is likely to be independent. If, on the other hand, one is governed solely by forces on the outside—cultural roles, the expectations and opinions of others—then one is less independent.

One's home address isn't the main issue. The main issue is, Do people listen to that important person inside—our truest self—that lovable bully and irritating pest who knows what is best for us, at least if we pay attention? Perhaps our greatest task as parents is to phase out as the lovable bullies and irritating pests in our childrens' lives and let their own inner voice take over.

So that's what I unlearned. What I learned, on the other hand, was provided by the people who talked with me or answered my survey. Their experiences were valuable in themselves and were also useful in helping me articulate what I knew from having so many young adults around the house at one time or another. If you've read this book through from start to finish, you know what I have learned. On the other hand, if you skipped to the end, to see how it all came out, the ending is as follows.

Launching a young person into adulthood can be even more rewarding than teaching children to talk or walk or ride a bicycle. Because it is finally the real life they've been waiting for. When kids are teetering on the edge of the nest, parents can teach them the most important of life's lessons, how to fend for themselves. But the ironic glory of nest-leaving is this: If the parents as life coaches do a good job of teaching independence, they draw closer to their children. Why? Because, through sensitive coaching, the parents clearly establish themselves as allies: supporters of the efforts and aspirations of their offspring. And who doesn't love an ally? Parental effort at this last stage of growing up often serves to forge strong lifelong bonds between the two generations.

The final blessed contradiction is this: To let them go is to get them back, this time as friends.

I'd like to leave you with a true story. . . .

There once was a conscientious mother who had six young adult children. One day, she was discussing her children's problems and her inadequacy as a mother with her priest/confessor. He listened for a while and then he said:

"Stop worrying about your children. After all, Jesus has already saved them, so you don't have to." He added, "And as your penance I want you and your husband to go to the beach with six balloons and release them one by one. Then do the same with the six people you brought into the world."

So the mother and father went to the beach and let the balloons float away into the sky one by one. And then they did the same with their six offspring.

Appendix A

Parent Survey

I sent this survey to parents of young adults. About five dozen individuals responded, often attaching comments that went beyond the sixteen pages of questions they had already answered. *Emptying the Nest* owes much to these generous mothers and fathers.

The survey was intended as an informal gauge of what some families are doing, thinking, and feeling on the subject of emptying the nest. It was not meant to be a broad scientific study that used a large number of parents from diverse socioeconomic and cultural backgrounds. I was looking not so much for statistical significance but for emotional truths and practical advice.

Dear Parent,

I'm writing a book about how to launch sons and

daughters into the adult world and would like to ask you about your experience in this last stage of child-raising. If you have at least one son or daughter who is out of school and on his or her own (more or less), I would appreciate your thoughts on how to best navigate this last part of parenthood. Other parents are often in the dark about how to best help the kids out of the nest. Your experience, good and bad, will help others find their way through these years.

If you have a young postschool adult living with you, I would appreciate hearing about that, too. Some people do well with this live-home arrangement. Others don't like it, so I'd like to find out what makes two-generational living together work in some cases and not in others.

As in my last book (*Schizophrenia: Straight Talk for Families and Friends*), I will keep all material confidential. When I use personal material in a book, I use no names, so you can say whatever is on your mind with confidence.

A stamped envelope is attached for your convenience. Thank you very much for participating. And please feel free to add your own comments and observations to this material.

Sincerely,

Maryellen Walsh

SECTION ONE: BASIC INFORMATION
  1. NAME AND ADDRESS (OPTIONAL)

2. YOUR AGE AND SEX   3. EDUCATION

4. OCCUPATION   5. MARITAL STATUS

6. AGE AND OCCUPATION OF OTHER PARENT

7. PLEASE TELL AGE AND SEX OF EACH OF YOUR
CHILDREN. USE THEIR NAMES TOO, IF IT'S EASIER
THAN TALKING ABOUT "CHILD NUMBER ONE"
AND "CHILD NUMBER TWO" AS INDICATED IN THE
CHART BELOW. THEN JUST TELL BRIEFLY WHERE
EACH IS LIVING AND WHAT EACH IS NOW DOING.

SEX AND AGE LIVES WHERE? DOES WHAT?

CHILD #1
CHILD #2
CHILD #3
CHILD #4
CHILD #5

8. WHAT DID EACH OF YOUR CHILDREN MAJOR IN?

9. IN YOUR OPINION, DID THEIR COLLEGE MAJORS
   BEAR ANY USEFUL RELATION TO THEIR FIRST
   JOBS? PLEASE GIVE SPECIFICS FOR EACH CHILD.

10. WHAT ROLE, IF ANY, DID YOU PLAY IN THE
    CHOICE OF THEIR COLLEGE MAJORS?

11. WHAT ROLE, IF ANY, DID YOU HAVE IN THEIR
    CHOICE OF A PROFESSION?

12. DID YOU ENCOURAGE THEM TO GO INTO A PAR-
    TICULAR PROFESSION?

13. DID ANY OF YOUR OFFSPRING HAVE DIFFICULTY
    DECIDING WHAT TO BE?

14. IF YES, HOW DID EACH RESOLVE THE DIFFICULTY?

15. DID ANY OF YOUR OFFSPRING HAVE TROUBLE
    FINDING THEIR FIRST ADULT JOBS?

16. IF THEY DID HAVE TROUBLE, IS THERE ANYTHING YOU OR THEY LEARNED FROM THAT EXPERIENCE THAT WOULD MAKE IT EASIER THE NEXT TIME?

17. HOW LONG DID EACH TAKE TO FIND A JOB?

18. DID THEY TAKE THEIR FIRST JOB OFFERS?

19. IF THEY DID TAKE THEIR FIRST OFFERS, DO YOU THINK IT WAS A GOOD IDEA? WHY OR WHY NOT?

20. WHAT ROLE DID YOU PLAY IN PURSUING YOUR OFFSPRINGS' FIRST FULL-TIME, "REAL" JOBS? FOR INSTANCE, DID YOU PROVIDE SPECIFIC HELP IN THE JOB-HUNTING PROCESS . . . SUCH AS EDITING RESUMES, GIVING LEADS, PLUGGING THEM INTO YOUR NETWORK OF FRIENDS AND BUSINESS ACQUAINTANCES?

21. WHAT NONPARENTAL HELP DID YOUR CHILDREN HAVE IN DETERMINING THEIR PROFESSIONS? FOR INSTANCE, DID THEY USE VOCATIONAL COUNSELING SERVICES IN COLLEGE?_____DID THEY USE A

PLACEMENT CENTER?_____WERE ANY OF YOUR OFFSPRING TESTED FOR VOCATIONAL APTITUDE? _____DID ANY ADULT, EITHER RELATIVE, FRIEND, OR TEACHER, COUNSEL AND ENCOURAGE THEM ABOUT THEIR FUTURES?_____PLEASE SPECIFY.

22. WHAT IS YOUR OPINION ABOUT VOCATIONAL COUNSELING IN THE SCHOOLS?

23. ABOUT HOW LONG DID EACH OF YOUR ADULT SONS AND DAUGHTERS STAY IN THEIR FIRST FULL-TIME JOBS?

24. IS IT EASY FOR YOU TO TALK TO YOUR CHILDREN ABOUT WHAT THEY DO FOR A LIVING?_____WHY OR WHY NOT?

25. HAVE ANY OF YOUR CHILDREN BEEN FIRED OR "LET GO"?

26. IF YES, HOW DID THEY AND YOU HANDLE IT?

27. DID ANY OF YOUR POSTSCHOOL KIDS GO THROUGH A "LAZY" PERIOD, WHERE THEY WEREN'T PURSUING JOB HUNTING WITH THE VIGOR YOU THOUGHT APPROPRIATE?

28. IF YES, PLEASE SAY A LITTLE ABOUT WHAT HAP-PENED, WHAT YOUR FEELINGS WERE, AND HOW THE SITUATION GOT RESOLVED.

29. WHAT, IN YOUR OPINION, MIGHT CAUSE OR CURE THIS "LAZINESS"? FOR INSTANCE, WHAT ADVICE WOULD YOU OFFER TO OTHER PARENTS WHO HAD A PROBLEM WITH A SON OR DAUGHTER WHO WOULDN'T GET OFF THE DIME?

30. ON THE OTHER HAND, DO YOU FEEL YOUR OFF-SPRING DEVOTE TOO MUCH TIME AND ENERGY TO THEIR WORK?_____IF YES, PLEASE GIVE AN EXAMPLE.

31. ARE YOU PLEASED WITH THE PROGRESS EACH OF YOUR OFFSPRING HAS MADE IN THE ADULT WORLD AS FAR AS JOBS GO? PLEASE EXPLAIN.

32. LOOKING AT YOUR OFFSPRING . . . CAN YOU SAY WHETHER THEY FEEL THEY ARE PURSUING MEAN-INGFUL LIFE WORK OR ARE THEY DISAPPOINTED IN WHAT THE WORK WORLD HAS TO OFFER?

33. WHAT, IN YOUR OPINION, ARE THE BIGGEST OBSTACLES TO YOUNG PEOPLE GETTING PROPERLY LAUNCHED INTO ADULTHOOD?

34. HAVE YOU EVER FELT THAT ANY OF YOUR CHIL-DREN TRIED TO BE THE EXACT OPPOSITE OF WHAT YOU, THE PARENT, WANTED? (FOR EXAMPLE, THINK OF RONALD REAGAN JUNIOR BECOMING A BALLET DANCER.)

35. IF YES, PLEASE GIVE THE EXAMPLE.

36. SOME KIDS THINK THEY HAVE TO BE PRESIDENT OF THE UNITED STATES OR GENERAL MOTORS TO BE WORTHWHILE PROFESSIONALLY. THIS OVER-AMBITION SEEMS TO BE A BIG OBSTACLE TO THE REALISTIC PURSUIT OF A CAREER. HAVE YOU FOUND THIS TO BE A PROBLEM?

37. HAS TOO LITTLE SELF-ESTEEM BEEN A PROBLEM?

38. IF YES, COULD YOU BRIEFLY DESCRIBE THE SITUATION?

39. AS FAR AS JOB HUNTING AND THE JOB MARKET GO, WOULD YOU WANT TO TRADE PLACES WITH YOUR KIDS?

40. WHY OR WHY NOT?

41. HOW HAS THE JOB-HUNTING ENVIRONMENT CHANGED SINCE YOU WERE FIRST OUT IN THE WORLD?

42. HAVE ANY OF YOUR POSTSCHOOL OFFSPRING DELAYED GETTING A "GROWN-UP JOB" WHILE THEY SKI-BUMMED, TRAVELED, OR DID SOME-THING THE WORLD THINKS IMPRACTICAL?

43. IF YES, DID YOU APPROVE, OPPOSE, OR HELP? PLEASE EXPLAIN.

44. DID YOU SUGGEST THE MILITARY OR GOVERN-MENT SERVICE SUCH AS THE PEACE CORPS? _____ IF YES, WHAT REACTION DID YOU GET?

45. ANY OTHER COMMENTS/TIPS ABOUT CHOOSING A PROFESSION/FINDING A JOB?

SECTION TWO: FINANCES

46. EARLY FINANCIAL EXPERIENCE.
WHAT WERE YOUR CHILDREN'S GROWING-UP EXPERIENCES WITH MONEY? FOR INSTANCE, DID THEY HAVE AN ALLOWANCE THEY HAD TO STICK TO? OR DID THEY ASK FOR MONEY WHEN THEY NEEDED IT?

47. HOW DID YOUR OFFSPRING BECOME FINANCIALLY WEANED FROM YOU? . . . OR IS THE FAMILY STILL PROVIDING SOME AID?

48. IF STILL PROVIDING AID, PLEASE INDICATE WHAT IT'S FOR . . . GENERAL LIVING EXPENSES? . . . OR SPECIFIC THINGS LIKE CAR INSURANCE/MEDICAL INSURANCE?

49. DOES "HELPING OUT" FINANCIALLY CAUSE FAMILY CONFLICT . . . FOR INSTANCE, MOM WANTING TO HELP THE KIDS OUT AND DAD WANTING TO GET THEM OFF THE PAYROLL?

50. IF THERE'S CONFLICT, HOW DOES IT GET RESOLVED?

51. SOME YOUNG PEOPLE COMPLAIN THAT THEIR PARENTS ARE NOT EVEN-HANDED IN THEIR FINANCIAL AID. FOR INSTANCE, PARENTS MAY HELP ONE OFFSPRING WHO'S STARTING A NEW BUSINESS, WHILE GIVING NOTHING TO ONE WHO'S WORKING FOR SOMEONE ELSE. HAVE YOU HAD THESE PROBLEMS WITH PERCEIVED "UNFAIRNESS"?

52. IF YES, PLEASE TELL WHAT THE PROBLEM WAS AND HOW IT DID OR DIDN'T GET RESOLVED.

53. IF YOU MAKE LOANS TO OFFSPRING, DO YOU WRITE AN AGREEMENT AS TO AMOUNT, TERMS, INTEREST, OR IS THE UNDERSTANDING MORE INFORMAL?

54. HAVE YOUR OFFSPRING REPAID LOANS AS AGREED?

55. IF NOT, WHAT, IF ANYTHING, WAS DONE?

56. HAVE YOU PROVIDED OR WOULD YOU PROVIDE TUITION FOR GRADUATE OR PROFESSIONAL SCHOOL?_____IF SO, AS A LOAN OR A GIFT?

57. IF YOU WERE FINANCING GRADUATE EDUCATION, WOULD YOU REQUIRE COPAYMENT, THAT IS, PER- HAPS GOING HALVES ON TUITION WITH A SON OR DAUGHTER WHO IS EARNING THE REST HIM/ HERSELF?

58. WHAT ABOUT HANDLING MONEY NOW? DO YOUR OFFSPRING HANDLE MONEY AND CREDIT WELL OR ARE THEY HAVING TROUBLE? PLEASE EXPLAIN.

59. DID YOU COSIGN THEIR FIRST CREDIT CARDS?

60. IF YES, WHAT WAS YOUR EXPERIENCE?

61. YOUR CONCLUSION?

62. HOW DID YOUR CHILDREN ACQUIRE THEIR FIRST CARS? DID YOU BUY THEM? DID THEY?

63. DO YOU EXPECT YOUR CHILDREN TO DO BETTER THAN YOU FINANCIALLY? ABOUT THE SAME? WORSE?

64. ANY COMMENTS/TIPS ABOUT FINANCES/MONEY HANDLING?

SECTION THREE: SHELTER

65. HELP WITH RENTING.

IF YOU HAVE OFFSPRING WHO RENT AN APART-
MENT OR HOUSE, PLEASE SAY A LITTLE ABOUT
WHAT HELP, IF ANY, YOU GAVE IN HOUSE OR
APARTMENT HUNTING. FOR INSTANCE, DID YOU
HELP WITH FIRST AND LAST MONTH'S RENT? WITH
OUTFITTING THE PLACE WITH FURNITURE OR
KITCHENWARE? WITH MOVING? WITH DECORAT-
ING? WITH DECIPHERING A LEASE? OR DID THEY
RELOCATE PRETTY MUCH BY THEMSELVES?

66. HELP WITH BUYING A HOME.
DO ANY OF YOUR OFFSPRING OWN A
HOME?_____IF YES, DID YOU HELP FINANCIAL-
LY?_____IF SO, HOW?

67. IF YES, WILL YOU SHARE IN THE EVENTUAL SALES
PROCEEDS?

68. DID YOU HAVE HELP FROM YOUR PARENTS IN BUY-
ING A HOME?

69. DID ANY OF YOUR OFFSPRING HAVE TROUBLE
WITH ROOMMATES? FOR INSTANCE, LIVING WITH
PEERS WHO WERE A BAD INFLUENCE AS FAR AS
DRUGS AND ALCOHOL WENT ... OR HAVING

ROOMMATES WHO RIPPED OFF YOUR OFFSPRING'S
MONEY OR POSSESSIONS?_____IF YES, WHAT WAS
THE NATURE OF THE PROBLEM AND HOW WAS IT
RESOLVED?

70. ON A LIGHTER NOTE, COULD YOU PASS ON A FEW
    TIPS FOR GOOD, EASY, INEXPENSIVE MEALS FOR
    YOUNG ADULTS TO MAKE AT HOME?

IF YOU'VE HAD A POSTCOLLEGE SON OR DAUGHTER
LIVING AT HOME FOR MORE THAN A FEW TRANSI-
TIONAL WEEKS, PLEASE ANSWER QUESTIONS 71
THROUGH 77 FOLLOWING. IF YOU HAVE NOT HAD A
POSTSCHOOL CHILD LIVING WITH YOU, PLEASE GO TO
QUESTION 78 IN THE NEXT SECTION, *HEALTH.*

71. ABOUT HOW LONG DID YOUR SON(S)/DAUGH-
    TER(S) LIVE WITH YOU AFTER THEY HAD FINISHED
    THEIR SCHOOLING?

72. WHAT WERE THE REWARDS OF THOSE ARRANGE-
    MENTS?

73. WHAT WERE THE DRAWBACKS OR PROBLEMS?

74. HOW WERE THE PROBLEMS HANDLED?

75. WHAT WERE THE REASONS FOR LIVING AT HOME? ECONOMIC? GOOD COMPANIONSHIP? NEAR WORK? HAD THE EXTRA ROOM? SOMEONE'S SPECIAL NEEDS?

76. DID YOU ENCOUNTER CRITICISM BECAUSE YOU STILL HAD CHILDREN AT HOME?____IF YES, FROM WHOM? . . . AND HOW DID YOU FEEL ABOUT BEING CRITICIZED?

77. IF YOUR OFFSPRING LEFT HOME SINCE LIVING WITH YOU, WHY DID THEY LEAVE?

SECTION FOUR: HEALTH

78. ARE YOUR POSTSCHOOL OFFSPRING COVERED BY MEDICAL INSURANCE?____IF SO, WHO PAYS FOR IT?

79. HAVE ANY OF THEM HAD SERIOUS HEALTH PROB-
LEMS?_____IF SO, WHAT CONSEQUENCES HAS
THIS HAD FOR YOU AND FOR THEM?

80. MENTAL ILLNESSES AND OTHER DISORDERS OF
BRAIN CHEMISTRY OFTEN APPEAR FOR THE FIRST
TIME IN YOUNG ADULTS. HAVE YOU ENCOUN-
TERED THESE PROBLEMS?

81. IF YES, COULD YOU SAY WHAT HAPPENED? FOR
INSTANCE, HOW WAS THE DISORDER DIAGNOSED,
TREATED, OR NOT TREATED? HOW DID IT AFFECT
YOU AND YOUR FAMILY?

82. WHAT WOULD YOU SAY ARE THE SIGNS OR SYMP-
TOMS OF MAJOR MENTAL ILLNESS?

83. MANY PARENTS HAVE PROBLEMS WITH THEIR OFF-
SPRING ABUSING DRUGS AND ALCOHOL. TO YOUR
KNOWLEDGE, HAVE ANY OF YOUR OFFSPRING
ABUSED DRUGS OR ALCOHOL?_____IF YES,
COULD YOU SAY WHAT HAPPENED OR IS HAP-
PENING?

84. WHAT RECOMMENDATIONS WOULD YOU HAVE FOR OTHER PARENTS WITH THESE PROBLEMS? PLEASE BE AS SPECIFIC AS YOU CAN, FOR INSTANCE, RECOMMENDING HELPFUL ORGANIZA- TIONS OR SPECIFIC PARENTAL BEHAVIOR.

85. WHAT WOULD YOU SAY ARE THE SIGNS OR SYMP- TOMS OF ALCOHOL ABUSE?

86. WHAT WOULD YOU SAY ARE THE SIGNS OR SYMP- TOMS OF DRUG ABUSE?

SECTION FIVE: PERSPECTIVE OVER TIME

87. WHAT WAS IT LIKE FOR YOU WHEN YOU LEFT HOME DECADES AGO?

88. HOW DOES THAT EXPERIENCE COMPARE WITH YOUR OWN OFFSPRING'S LEAVING THE NEST? FOR INSTANCE, WHAT DIFFERENCES ARE THERE BETWEEN GENERATIONS? WHAT SIMILARITIES?

89. IN YOUR OPINION, ARE THE CHANGES IN THE GROWING-UP PROCESS OVER THE LAST DECADE FOR THE BETTER? PLEASE TELL WHY OR WHY NOT.

90. WHAT PROBLEMS OR TRIUMPHS DO YOU SPECIFI- CALLY REMEMBER ENCOUNTERING WHEN YOU WERE YOUNG AND LEAVING HOME?

91. HOW DID YOUR PARENTS HELP OR HINDER YOU IN LEAVING THE NEST?

SECTION SIX: RECENT PARENT EXPERIENCE AND OPINION

92. WHAT EMOTIONS DID YOU FEEL WHEN A CHILD LEFT THE NEST?

93. HAS THE NEST LEAVING AFFECTED YOUR RELA- TIONSHIP WITH YOUR MATE? IF YES, HOW?

94. HAS THE NEST-LEAVING EXPERIENCE AFFECTED

YOUR PROFESSIONAL OR VOLUNTEER LIFE? FOR
INSTANCE, DO YOU DEVOTE MORE TIME TO
ACHIEVING YOUR OWN GOALS?

95. IF SPENDING MORE TIME ON OWN GOALS, WHAT
RESULTS HAVE YOU GOTTEN AND ARE THEY SAT-
ISFACTORY TO YOU?

96. IF YOU ACHIEVED SOMETHING YOU FEEL WAS
UNUSUALLY POSITIVE AND WORTHWHILE,
WOULD YOU LIKE BEING INTERVIEWED BY PHONE
OR IN PERSON ABOUT YOUR LIFE?

97. PLEASE INCLUDE YOUR PHONE NUMBER HERE IF
YOU WOULD LIKE TO CONTRIBUTE YOUR EXPE-
RIENCE.

98. HAS THE EXPERIENCE OF CHILDREN LEAVING
HOME HAD NEGATIVE RESULTS?____FOR
INSTANCE, HAS THE MEANING OF YOUR LIFE
DIMINISHED?

99. WHAT WOULD BE YOUR ADVICE TO OTHER PARENTS APPROACHING THIS STAGE OF THEIR LIVES?

100. LOOKING BACK, WHAT WERE YOUR BIGGEST SUCCESSES WITH YOUR KIDS?

101. BIGGEST MISTAKES WITH THEM?—OR PUT MORE POSITIVELY—WHAT DO YOU WISH YOU HAD DONE DIFFERENTLY?

102. WHAT DO YOUR KIDS ESPECIALLY APPRECIATE ABOUT YOU?

103. WHAT DO YOU ESPECIALLY APPRECIATE ABOUT THEM?

104. WHAT WAS THE NICEST THING ANY OF YOUR KIDS DID FOR YOU?

105. WHAT DO THEY CRITICIZE YOU FOR?

106. AND WHAT DO YOU WISH WERE DIFFERENT ABOUT THEM?

107. HOW WOULD YOU CHARACTERIZE YOUR RELA-TIONSHIP WITH THEM NOW? FOR INSTANCE, DO YOU FEEL VERY CLOSE TO THEM, HAVE FREQUENT POSITIVE CONVERSATIONS, AND SO ON? OR DO YOU FEEL MORE DISTANT, JUST SEEING THEM ON SPECIAL OCCASIONS?

108. WHAT VALUES DO YOU WANT TO PASS ON TO THEM?

109. DO THEY SHOW SIGNS OF HAVING EMBRACED THESE VALUES?_____IF YES, COULD YOU GIVE AN EXAMPLE?

110. WHAT FAMILY TRADITIONS WOULD YOU LIKE TO PASS ON? FOR INSTANCE, ARE THERE NICE HOLI-DAY TRADITIONS OR TRADITIONS OF DAILY LIV-ING THAT YOU WOULD LIKE TO SEE YOUR CHILDREN ADOPT?

111. IF YES, CAN YOU BRIEFLY DESCRIBE THEM?

112. AROUND THE TIME OF NEST LEAVING, WHAT EXPERIENCE UPSET YOU THE MOST, MADE YOU MOST ANGRY OR MOST WORRIED?

113. AROUND THE TIME OF LEAVING THE NEST, WHAT EXPERIENCE WAS THE MOST SATISFYING?

114. IF YOU HAD TO GIVE ADVICE TO OTHER PARENTS ABOUT MAINTAINING GOOD COMMUNICATION WITH THEIR YOUNG ADULTS, WHAT WOULD YOU TELL THEM?

115. DO YOU FEEL THERE IS A "VALUES GAP" BETWEEN YOU AND YOUR CHILDREN? THAT IS, DO YOU CHERISH DIFFERENT THINGS, HAVE DIFFERENT GOALS, SEE THE WORLD DIFFERENTLY?

116. IF YOU FEEL THERE IS A VALUES GAP, COULD YOU DESCRIBE IT BRIEFLY?

117. WHAT MIGHT BE THE BEST WAY TO OVERCOME SUCH A GAP?

118. WHAT UNITES YOU WITH YOUR CHILDREN?

119. ARE GIRLS EASIER TO LAUNCH THAN BOYS, VICE VERSA, OR NO DIFFERENCE?

120. WOULD YOU GIVE YOUR DEFINITION OF BEING TRULY GROWN UP?

121. IN YOUR OPINION, WHAT ARE THE MOST HELPFUL THINGS A PARENT CAN DO TO LAUNCH OFF-SPRING SUCCESSFULLY INTO ADULT LIFE?

122. DO YOU FEEL YOU "SPOILED" YOUR KIDS?

123. IF YES, HOW? AND WITH WHAT RESULTS

124. IF YOU THINK YOU SPOILED THEM, WOULD YOU TREAT THEM DIFFERENTLY NOW? PLEASE EXPLAIN.

125. WOULD YOU DESCRIBE YOUR PARENTING STYLE AS STRICT, VERY LAID-BACK, OR SOMEWHERE IN THE MIDDLE?

126. HAVE YOU EVER HAD TO HAVE A SHOWDOWN WITH YOUR KIDS TO GET THEM OUT OF THE NEST?

127. IF YES, PLEASE TELL WHAT HAPPENED, HOW YOU FELT, AND IF YOU WOULD DO IT THE SAME WAY AGAIN.

128. IS THERE SOMETHING I SHOULD HAVE ASKED YOU THAT I DIDN'T?

THANK YOU VERY MUCH FOR YOUR PARTICIPATION. AGAIN, IF YOU HAVE OTHER THOUGHTS, PLEASE ENCLOSE THEM IN THE ADDRESSED AND STAMPED ENVELOPE ATTACHED TO THIS SURVEY.

Appendix B

Further Reading

Ashton, Betty. *Betty Ashton's Guide to Living on Your Own*. Boston: Little, Brown, 1988.

Bambridge, B. "Injury Time." In *The Best of Modern Humor*, ed. M. Richler. New York: Knopf, 1983.

Beattie, Melody. *Codependent No More*. Center City, Minn.: Hazelden Foundation, 1987.

Bolles, R. *The 1988 What Color Is Your Parachute?* Berkeley: Ten Speed Press, 1988.

Brans, J. *Mother, I Have Something to Tell You*. New York: Signet, 1987.

Dight, J., *Do Your Parents Drive You Crazy?* New York: Prentice Hall Press, 1987.

"The Downwardly Mobile Baby-Boomers," *Wall Street Journal*, February 12, 1985.

Edelhart, M. *Getting from Twenty to Thirty*. New York: M. Evans and Co., 1983.

Erikson, E., ed. *Adulthood*. New York: W. W. Norton, 1978.

Falvey, J. *After College: The Business of Getting Jobs*. Charlotte, Vt.: Williamson Publishing, 1986.

French, M. *Her Mother's Daughter.* New York: Ballantine, 1987.

Gilligan, C. *In a Different Voice: Psychological Theory and Women's Development.* Cambridge, Mass.: Harvard University Press, 1982.

Glick, P., and S. Lin. "More Young Adults Living with Their Parents: Who Are They?" *Journal of Marriage and the Family* 48:107–112 (1986).

Gold, M., *The Facts About Drugs and Alcohol.* New York: Bantam, 1989.

Goldscheider, F., and J. DaVanzo. "Living Arrangements and the Transition to Adulthood." *Demography* 22:545–563 (1985).

Goldscheider, C., and F. Goldscheider. "Moving Out and Marriage: What Do Young Adults Expect?" *American Sociological Review* 52:278–285 (1987).

Goldscheider, F., and C. LeBourdais. "The Decline in Age at Leaving Home, 1920–1979." *Sociology and Social Research* 70:143–145 (1986).

Goldscheider, F., and L. Waite. "Nest-Leaving Patterns and the Transition to Marriage for Young Men and Women." *Journal of Marriage and the Family* 49:507–516 (1987).

Gould, R. *Transformations: Growth and Change in Adult Life.* New York: Touchstone, 1979.

Grigsby, J., and J. McGowan. "Still in the Nest: Adult Children Living with Their Parents." *Sociology and Social Research* 70:146–148 (1986).

Half, R. *The Robert Half Way to Get Hired in Today's Job Market.* New York: Bantam, 1983.

Heer, D., R. Hodge, and M. Felson. "The Cluttered Nest: Evidence That Young Adults Are More Likely to Live at Home Now Than in Recent Past." *Sociology and Social Research* 69: 436–441 (1985).

Hodgson, H. *A Parent's Survival Guide: How to Cope When Your Kid Is Using Drugs.* New York: Harper/Hazelden, 1986.

Kett, J., *Rites of Passage: Adolescence in America 1790 to the Present.* New York: Basic Books, 1977.

Leape, M., and S. Vacca. *The Harvard Guide to Careers.* Cambridge; Mass.: Harvard University Press, 1987.

Appendix B

Levering, R., M. Moskowitz, and M. Katz. *The Hundred Best Companies to Work for in America*. Reading, Mass.: Addison-Wesley, 1984.

Littwin, S. *The Postponed Generation: Why American Youth Are Growing Up Later*. New York: William Morrow, 1986.

Merser, C. *"Grown-Ups": A Generation in Search of Adulthood*. New York: G. P. Putnam's Sons, 1987.

Okimoto, J., and P. Stegall. *Boomerang Kids: How to Live with Adult Children Who Return Home*. Boston: Little, Brown, 1987.

"Parenthood II: When a Nest Won't Stay Empty." *New York Times*, March 12, 1987.

Schnaiberg, A., and S. Goldenberg. "From Empty Nest to Crowded Nest: The Dynamics of Incompletely Launched Young Adults." *Social Problems* 36: 251–269.

Sheehy, G. *Passages: Predictable Crises of Adult Life*. New York: Bantam, 1985.

Shehan, C., F. Berardo, and D. Berardo. "The Empty Nest Is Full Again: Implications for Parent–Child Relations." *Parenting Studies* 1:67–73 (1984).

Sher, Barbara and Annie Gottlieb. *Wishcraft: How to Get What You Really Want*. New York: Viking, 1979.

"Snapshot of a Changing America." *Time*, September 2, 1985.

Springhill, J. *Coming of Age: Adolescence in Britain, 1869–1960*. Dublin: Gill and Macmillan Ltd., 1986.

Stevens-Long, J. *Adult Life: Developmental Processes*. Palo Alto, Calif.: Mayfield Publishing, 1984.

Walsh, Maryellen. *Schizophrenia: Straight Talk for Families and Friends*. New York: William Morrow, 1985.

Webb, M., "Back to the Nest." *New York Magazine*, February 1, 1987.

Wein, S. *Wing Walking: A Totally Different Approach to the Job Market*. San Francisco: Alchemy Press, 1984.

York, P., D. York, and T. Wachtel. *Toughlove*. New York: Bantam, 1983.

Index

Index

manners for, *see* Manners
  as obstacle to leaving nest, 21
  prejudices of, about jobs, 61–64
  responses of, to survey, 44–48
  single, 49–51
Parent-initiated conversations,
  about careers, 65–66
Parent survey, 154–178
  basic information in, 155–163
  finances in, 163–166
  health in, 169–171
  perspective over time in, 171–172
  recent parent experience and
    opinion in, 172–178
  shelter in, 166–169
Partner, agreement with, on main
  issues, 36–37
Perspective over time, in parent survey, 171–172
Phone, and job hunt, 71
Plaid dad, 41–42
Power, changing, 132–134
Prejudices of parents, about jobs,
  61–64
Presents, college graduation, 88; *see
  also* Gifts
Privacy, 37–38
Professional incompetents, 124
Protocol, changing, 132–134
"Pull-aparts" of living together,
  agreement on handling of,
  30–32

Questions, gently prodding, 15–16

References
  for apartment application, 99–
    100
  in job hunt, 75–76
Reflection, of thoughts and feelings,
  16
Rejection, in job hunt, 71
Relations, family, 4, 129–149
Relationships, romantic, of offspring, manners and, 147–
  148
Rent, 89
Rescuing offspring, 16–18
Respect, of own feelings on sex
  partner/sleep-over issue, 32–
  33

Responsibility(ies)
  authority equal to, 43–44
  household, agreement on and
    enforcement of, 33–34, 46
Resumes, 72–77
Right way to grow up, 8–9
Role models, 66
Roles, in family, 41–44
Romantic relationships of offspring,
  manners and, 147–148
Roommate(s)
  coed, 102–103
  financial responsibility and, 99

San Jose State University, 67
Schizophrenia, 120, 121–123
*Schizophrenia: Straight Talk for Fami-
  lies and Friends*, 123, 155
Schnaiberg, Allan, 16–17, 39
Self-knowledge, and career, 65–68
Senior year in high school, 11–12
Sexual drive, 5–6
Sexual sleep-overs, 148
  respect of own feelings on, 32–33
Shakespeare, xix
Shelter, in parent survey, 166–169;
  see also Apartment hunting
  and living; Housing costs
Sher, Barbara, 81
Single parent, 49–51
Sleep-overs, sexual, 148
  respect of own feelings on, 32–33
Small companies, in job hunt, 72
Smoking, 30–31
Snyder, John, xix
Space
  in job hunt, 71
  as problem in living at home, 47
Spouse, agreement with, on main
  issues, 36–37
Stanford Medical Center, 109
"Stupid" money, 93–94
Support
  moral, 12–16
  of someone who is supporting
    nonworking mate, 90
Survey, parent, *see* Parent survey

Talking
  chemical abuse and, 113–114
  in resolution of difficulties, 47–48

187

Index

ABOUT THE AUTHOR

MARYELLEN WALSH is the author of another self-help book for families, *Schizophrenia: Straight Talk for Families and Friends*. She has emptied the nest of three sons and one daughter and lives in Silicon Valley, south of San Francisco, writing nonfiction, fiction, and a newspaper column.